THE
AI
REVOLUTION

AI . II REVOLUTIO:

UNDERSTANDING, ITS IMPACT, AND THE FUTURE OF HUMANITY

THE AI REVOLUTION

Credits & Foreword AI is not just a technological advancement—it is a revolution redefining humanity's place in the digital age. Its presence is felt in every aspect of life, from the way we work to the way we interact, reshaping the very fabric of society. Understanding AI means understanding the future, and those who harness its potential will shape the course of history. The evolution of AI is not just a technical shift; it is a societal transformation. Throughout history, we have witnessed how revolutions in technology reshape civilization—from the steam engine to the internet. AI follows this trajectory, with the potential to redefine what it means to be human. Every industry, from healthcare to finance, is being disrupted, forcing humanity to adapt in unprecedented ways. The coming decades will determine whether AI remains a tool for prosperity or becomes an uncontrollable force.

Credits AI is not just a technological advancement—it is a revolution redefining humanity's place in the digital age. Its presence is felt in every aspect of life, from the way we work to the way we interact, reshaping the very fabric of society. Understanding AI means understanding the future, and those who harness its potential will

shape the course of history. The evolution of AI is not just a technical shift; it is a societal transformation. Throughout history, we have witnessed how revolutions in technology reshape civilization—from the steam engine to the internet. AI follows this trajectory, with the potential to redefine what it means to be human. Every industry, from healthcare to finance, is being disrupted, forcing humanity to adapt in unprecedented ways. The coming decades will determine whether AI remains a tool for prosperity or becomes an uncontrollable force.

Author: John Smedley
Publication Year: 2025 AI is not just a technological advancement—it is a revolution redefining humanity's place in the digital age. Its presence is felt in every aspect of life, from the way we work to the way we interact, reshaping the very fabric of society. Understanding AI means understanding the future, and those who harness its potential will shape the course of history. The evolution of AI is not just a technical shift; it is a societal transformation. Throughout history, we have witnessed how revolutions in technology reshape civilization—from the steam engine to the internet. AI follows this trajectory, with the potential to redefine what it means to be human. Every industry, from healthcare to finance, is being disrupted, forcing humanity to adapt in unprecedented ways. The coming decades will determine whether AI remains a tool for prosperity or becomes an uncontrollable force.

This book is a culmination of research, analysis, and AI-assisted content generation. Special thanks to the pioneers of artificial intelligence and the experts who have shaped the AI landscape. AI is not just a technological advancement—it is a revolution redefining humanity's place in the digital age. Its presence is felt in every aspect of life, from the way we work to the way we interact, reshaping the very fabric of society. Understanding AI means understanding the future, and those who harness its potential will shape the course of history.

--- AI is not just a technological advancement—it is a revolution redefining humanity's place in the digital age. Its presence is felt in every aspect of life, from the way we work to the way we interact, reshaping the very fabric of society. Understanding AI means understanding the future, and those who harness its potential will shape the course of history. The evolution of AI is not just a technical shift; it is a societal transformation. Throughout history, we have witnessed how revolutions in technology reshape civilization—from the steam engine to the internet. AI follows this trajectory, with the potential to redefine what it means to be human. Every industry, from healthcare to finance, is being disrupted, forcing humanity to adapt in unprecedented ways. The coming decades will determine whether AI remains a tool for prosperity or becomes an uncontrollable force.

Foreword AI is not just a technological advancement—it is a revolution redefining humanity's place in the digital age. Its presence is felt in every aspect of life, from the way we work to the way we interact, reshaping the very fabric of society. Understanding AI means understanding the future, and those who harness its potential will shape the course of history. The evolution of AI is not just a technical shift; it is a societal transformation. Throughout history, we have witnessed how revolutions in technology reshape civilization—from the steam engine to the internet. AI follows this trajectory, with the potential to redefine what it means to be human. Every industry, from healthcare to finance, is being disrupted, forcing humanity to adapt in unprecedented ways. The coming decades will determine whether AI remains a tool for prosperity or becomes an uncontrollable force.

Artificial Intelligence has rapidly evolved from a futuristic concept into a transformative force reshaping every aspect of human civilization. This book explores AI's impact on industries, creativity, ethics, and the future of intelligence. As AI continues to advance, we must carefully navigate its integration into society, ensuring that it serves as a tool for progress rather than disruption. The evolution of AI is not just a technical shift; it is a societal transformation. Throughout history, we have witnessed how revolutions in technology reshape civilization— from the steam engine to the internet. AI follows this trajectory, with the potential to redefine what it means to be human. Every industry, from healthcare to finance, is being disrupted, forcing humanity to adapt in unprecedented ways. The coming decades will determine whether AI remains a tool for prosperity or becomes an uncontrollable force.

The AI revolution is not an event in the distant future—it is happening now. The insights presented here aim to guide individuals, businesses, and policymakers toward an AI-powered world that benefits all of humanity. AI is not just a technological advancement—it is a revolution redefining humanity's place in the digital age. Its presence is felt in every aspect of life, from the way we work to the way we interact, reshaping the very fabric of society. Understanding AI means understanding the future, and those who harness its potential will shape the course of history.

--- AI is not just a technological advancement—it is a revolution redefining humanity's place in the digital age. Its presence is felt in every aspect of life, from the way we work to the way we interact, reshaping the very fabric of society. Understanding AI means understanding the future, and those who harness its potential will shape the course of history. The evolution of AI is not just a technical shift; it is a societal transformation. Throughout history, we have witnessed how revolutions in technology reshape civilization—from the steam engine to the internet. AI follows this trajectory, with the potential to redefine what it means to be human. Every industry, from healthcare to finance, is being disrupted, forcing humanity to adapt in unprecedented ways. The coming decades will determine whether AI remains a tool for prosperity or becomes an uncontrollable force.

Table of Contents

AI is not just a technological advancement—it is a revolution redefining humanity's place in the digital age. Its presence is felt in every aspect of life, from the way we work to the way we interact, reshaping the very fabric of society. Understanding AI means understanding the future, and those who harness its potential will shape the course of history. The evolution of AI is not just a technical shift; it is a societal transformation. Throughout history, we have witnessed how revolutions in technology reshape civilization—from the steam engine to the internet. AI follows this trajectory, with the potential to redefine what it means to be human. Every industry, from healthcare to finance, is being disrupted, forcing humanity to adapt in unprecedented ways. The coming decades will determine whether AI remains a tool for prosperity or becomes an uncontrollable force.

1. Credits & Foreword
2. Chapter 1: Introduction to AI
3. Chapter 2: The History of AI
4. Chapter 3: AI Today – Where We Stand
5. Chapter 4: Making Money with AI
6. Chapter 5: AI and the Human Mind
7. Chapter 6: The Future of AI
8. Chapter 7: Final Thoughts and The AI-Driven Future

--- AI is not just a technological advancement—it is a revolution redefining humanity's place in the digital age. Its presence is felt in every aspect of life, from the way we work to the way we interact, reshaping the very fabric of society. Understanding AI means understanding the future, and those who harness its potential will shape the course of history. The evolution of AI is not just a technical shift; it is a societal transformation. Throughout history, we have witnessed how revolutions in technology reshape civilization—from the steam engine to the internet. AI follows this trajectory, with the potential to redefine what it means to be human. Every industry, from healthcare to finance, is being disrupted, forcing humanity to adapt in unprecedented ways. The coming decades will determine whether AI remains a tool for prosperity or becomes an uncontrollable force.

CHAPTER 1: INTRODUCTION TO AI

What is Artificial Intelligence? AI is not just a technological advancement—it is a revolution redefining humanity's place in the digital age. Its presence is felt in every aspect of life, from the way we work to the way we interact, reshaping the very fabric of society. Understanding AI means understanding the future, and those who harness its potential will shape the course of history. The evolution of AI is not just a technical shift; it is a societal transformation. Throughout history, we have witnessed how revolutions in technology reshape civilization—from the steam engine to the internet. AI follows this trajectory, with the potential to redefine what it means to be human. Every industry, from healthcare to finance, is being disrupted, forcing humanity to adapt in unprecedented ways. The coming decades will determine whether AI remains a tool for prosperity or becomes an uncontrollable force.

Artificial Intelligence (AI) refers to the development of computer systems that can perform tasks typically requiring human intelligence. These tasks include reasoning, learning, problem-solving, perception, and language understanding. AI is transforming industries, enhancing decision-making, and shaping the future of human civilization. The evolution of AI is not just a technical shift; it is a societal transformation. Throughout history, we have witnessed how revolutions in technology reshape civilization—from the steam engine to the internet. AI follows this trajectory, with the potential to redefine what it means to be human. Every industry, from healthcare to finance, is being disrupted, forcing humanity to adapt in unprecedented ways. The coming decades will determine whether AI remains a tool for prosperity or becomes an uncontrollable force.

The Different Types of AI AI is not just a technological advancement—it is a revolution redefining humanity's place in the digital age. Its presence is felt in every aspect of life, from the way we work to the way we interact, reshaping the very fabric of society. Understanding AI means understanding the future, and those who harness its potential will shape the course of history. The evolution of AI is not just a technical shift; it is a societal transformation. Throughout history, we have witnessed how revolutions in technology reshape civilization—from the steam engine to the internet. AI follows this trajectory, with the potential to redefine what it means to be human. Every industry, from healthcare to finance, is being disrupted, forcing humanity to adapt in unprecedented ways. The coming decades will determine whether AI remains a tool for prosperity or becomes an uncontrollable force.

AI can be categorized into three main types: AI is not just a technological advancement—it is a revolution redefining humanity's place in the digital age. Its presence is felt in every aspect of life, from the way we work to the way we interact, reshaping the very fabric of society. Understanding AI means understanding the future, and those who harness its potential will shape the course of history. The evolution of AI is not just a technical shift; it is a societal transformation. Throughout history, we have witnessed how revolutions in technology reshape civilization—from the steam engine to the internet. AI follows this trajectory, with the potential to redefine what it means to be human. Every industry, from healthcare to finance, is being disrupted, forcing humanity to adapt in unprecedented ways. The coming decades will determine whether AI remains a tool for prosperity or becomes an uncontrollable force.

1. **Narrow AI (Weak AI)** – AI designed for specific tasks, such as voice assistants (Siri, Alexa) and recommendation algorithms.
2. **General AI (Strong AI)** – AI that can perform any intellectual task a human can do (currently theoretical).
3. **Superintelligent AI** – Hypothetical AI surpassing human intelligence in all aspects. The evolution of AI is not just a technical shift; it is a societal transformation. Throughout history, we have witnessed how revolutions in technology reshape civilization—from the steam engine to the internet. AI follows this trajectory, with the potential to redefine what it means to be human. Every industry, from healthcare to finance, is being disrupted,

forcing humanity to adapt in unprecedented ways. The coming decades will determine whether AI remains a tool for prosperity or becomes an uncontrollable force.

The Role of AI in Daily Life AI is not just a technological advancement—it is a revolution redefining humanity's place in the digital age. Its presence is felt in every aspect of life, from the way we work to the way we interact, reshaping the very fabric of society. Understanding AI means understanding the future, and those who harness its potential will shape the course of history. The evolution of AI is not just a technical shift; it is a societal transformation. Throughout history, we have witnessed how revolutions in technology reshape civilization—from the steam engine to the internet. AI follows this trajectory, with the potential to redefine what it means to be human. Every industry, from healthcare to finance, is being disrupted, forcing humanity to adapt in unprecedented ways. The coming decades will determine whether AI remains a tool for prosperity or becomes an uncontrollable force.

AI is embedded in modern society, influencing everything from communication to business operations: AI is not just a technological advancement—it is a revolution redefining humanity's place in the digital age. Its presence is felt in every aspect of life, from the way we work to the way we interact, reshaping the very fabric of society. Understanding AI means understanding the future, and those who harness its potential will shape the course of history. The evolution of AI is not just a technical shift; it is a societal transformation. Throughout history, we have witnessed how revolutions in technology reshape civilization—from the steam engine to the internet. AI follows this trajectory, with the potential to redefine what it means to be human. Every industry, from healthcare to finance, is being disrupted, forcing humanity to adapt in unprecedented ways. The coming decades will determine whether AI remains a tool for prosperity or becomes an uncontrollable force.

- **Virtual Assistants:** AI-driven chatbots and personal assistants automate customer service and productivity tasks.
- **Healthcare:** AI assists in diagnosing diseases and personalizing treatments.
- **Finance:** AI algorithms optimize trading, fraud detection, and risk assessment.
- **Transportation:** AI powers autonomous vehicles and smart traffic management.
- **Entertainment:** AI curates personalized content on platforms like Netflix and YouTube. AI is not just a technological advancement—it is a revolution redefining humanity's place in the digital age. Its presence is felt in every aspect of life, from the way we work to the way we interact, reshaping the very fabric of society. Understanding AI means

understanding the future, and those who harness its potential will shape the course of history. The evolution of AI is not just a technical shift; it is a societal transformation. Throughout history, we have witnessed how revolutions in technology reshape civilization—from the steam engine to the internet. AI follows this trajectory, with the potential to redefine what it means to be human. Every industry, from healthcare to finance, is being disrupted, forcing humanity to adapt in unprecedented ways. The coming decades will determine whether AI remains a tool for prosperity or becomes an uncontrollable force.

Key AI Breakthroughs AI is not just a technological advancement—it is a revolution redefining humanity's place in the digital age. Its presence is felt in every aspect of life, from the way we work to the way we interact, reshaping the very fabric of society. Understanding AI means understanding the future, and those who harness its potential will shape the course of history. The evolution of AI is not just a technical shift; it is a societal transformation. Throughout history, we have witnessed how revolutions in technology reshape civilization—from the steam engine to the internet. AI follows this trajectory, with the potential to redefine what it means to be human. Every industry, from healthcare to finance, is being disrupted, forcing humanity to adapt in unprecedented ways. The coming decades will determine whether AI remains a tool for prosperity or becomes an uncontrollable force.

AI has progressed rapidly, leading to groundbreaking innovations: AI is not just a technological advancement—it is a revolution redefining humanity's place in the digital age. Its presence is felt in every aspect of life, from the way we work to the way we interact, reshaping the very fabric of society. Understanding AI means understanding the future, and those who harness its potential will shape the course of history. The evolution of AI is not just a technical shift; it is a societal transformation. Throughout history, we have witnessed how revolutions in technology reshape civilization—from the steam engine to the internet. AI follows this trajectory, with the potential to redefine what it means to be human. Every industry, from healthcare to finance, is being disrupted, forcing humanity to adapt in unprecedented ways. The coming decades will determine whether AI remains a tool for prosperity or becomes an uncontrollable force.

- **1950s-1970s:** The birth of AI as an academic field, led by Alan Turing and John McCarthy.
- **1997:** IBM's Deep Blue defeats chess champion Garry Kasparov.
- **2011:** IBM Watson wins Jeopardy! against human champions.
- **2016:** AlphaGo beats the world champion in the complex board game Go.
- **2020s:** Generative AI models, such as GPT-4 and DALL·E, revolutionize creative industries. AI is not just a technological advancement—it is a revolution redefining humanity's place in the digital age. Its presence is felt in every aspect of life, from the way we work to the way we interact, reshaping the very fabric of society. Understanding AI means understanding the future, and those who harness its potential will shape the course of history. The evolution of AI is not just a technical shift; it is a societal transformation. Throughout history, we have witnessed how revolutions in technology reshape civilization—from the steam engine to the internet. AI follows this trajectory, with the potential to redefine what it means to be human. Every industry, from healthcare to finance, is being disrupted, forcing humanity to adapt in unprecedented ways. The coming decades will determine whether AI remains a tool for prosperity or becomes an uncontrollable force.

The Impact of AI on Society AI is not just a technological advancement—it is a revolution redefining humanity's place in the digital age. Its presence is felt in every aspect of life, from the way we work to the way we interact, reshaping the very fabric of society. Understanding AI means understanding the future, and those who harness its potential will shape the course of history. The evolution of AI is not just a technical shift; it is a societal transformation. Throughout history, we have witnessed how revolutions in technology reshape civilization—from the steam engine to the internet. AI follows this trajectory, with the potential to redefine what it means to be human. Every industry, from healthcare to finance, is being disrupted, forcing humanity to adapt in unprecedented ways. The coming decades will determine whether AI remains a tool for prosperity or becomes an uncontrollable force.

AI is not just a technological evolution—it is a fundamental shift in human capabilities. It is being used to streamline workflows, increase efficiency, and tackle complex challenges in science, medicine, and global economies. However, AI's influence extends beyond mere automation. It is shaping new forms of interaction between humans and machines, transforming social behaviors, and even altering philosophical debates on intelligence. The evolution of AI is not just a technical shift; it is a societal transformation. Throughout history, we have witnessed how revolutions in technology reshape civilization—from the steam engine to the internet. AI follows this trajectory, with the potential to redefine what it means to be human. Every industry, from healthcare to finance, is being disrupted, forcing humanity to adapt in unprecedented ways. The coming decades will determine whether AI remains a tool for prosperity or becomes an uncontrollable force.

One key area of AI's impact is in **human augmentation**. AI-powered prosthetics and brain-computer interfaces (BCIs) are pushing the boundaries of what it means to be human. In education, AI-driven tutoring systems provide students with personalized learning experiences, adapting to their needs in real time. The evolution of AI is not just a technical shift; it is a societal transformation. Throughout history, we have witnessed how revolutions in technology reshape civilization—from the steam engine to the internet. AI follows this trajectory, with the potential to redefine what it means to be human. Every industry, from healthcare to finance, is being disrupted, forcing humanity to adapt in unprecedented ways. The coming decades will determine whether AI remains a tool for prosperity or becomes an uncontrollable force.

Ethical Considerations in AI Development AI is not just a technological advancement—it is a revolution redefining humanity's place in the digital age. Its presence is felt in every aspect of life, from the way we work to the way we interact, reshaping the very fabric of society. Understanding AI means understanding the future, and those who harness its potential will shape the course of history. The evolution of AI is not just a technical shift; it is a societal transformation. Throughout history, we have witnessed how revolutions in technology reshape civilization—from the steam engine to the internet. AI follows this trajectory, with the potential to redefine what it means to be human. Every industry, from healthcare to finance, is being disrupted, forcing humanity to adapt in unprecedented ways. The coming decades will determine whether AI remains a tool for prosperity or becomes an uncontrollable force.

With AI's rapid growth come critical ethical considerations: AI is not just a technological advancement—it is a revolution redefining humanity's place in the digital age. Its presence is felt in every aspect of life, from the way we work to the way we interact, reshaping the very fabric of society. Understanding AI means understanding the future, and those who harness its potential will shape the course of history. The evolution of AI is not just a technical shift; it is a societal transformation. Throughout history, we have witnessed how revolutions in technology reshape civilization—from the steam engine to the internet. AI follows this trajectory, with the potential to redefine what it means to be human. Every industry, from healthcare to finance, is being disrupted, forcing humanity to adapt in unprecedented ways. The coming decades will determine whether AI remains a tool for prosperity or becomes an uncontrollable force.

- **Bias in AI Algorithms:** AI models can inherit biases from training data, leading to discrimination.
- **Privacy Concerns:** AI-powered surveillance raises questions about personal data security.
- **Automation and Job Displacement:** AI-driven automation may replace traditional jobs, requiring workforce adaptation.
- **AI in Warfare:** Autonomous weapons and AI-driven cyber warfare pose significant risks. AI is not just a technological advancement—it is a revolution redefining humanity's place in the digital age. Its presence is felt in every aspect of life, from the way we work to the way we interact, reshaping the very fabric of society. Understanding AI means understanding the future, and those who harness its potential will shape the course of history. The evolution of AI is not just a technical shift; it is a societal transformation. Throughout history, we have witnessed how revolutions in technology reshape civilization—from the steam engine to the internet. AI follows this trajectory, with the potential to redefine what it means to be human. Every industry, from healthcare to finance, is being disrupted, forcing humanity to adapt in unprecedented ways. The coming decades will determine whether AI remains a tool for prosperity or becomes an uncontrollable force.

The Future of AI AI is not just a technological advancement—it is a revolution redefining humanity's place in the digital age. Its presence is felt in every aspect of life, from the way we work to the way we interact, reshaping the very fabric of society. Understanding AI means understanding the future, and those who harness its potential will shape the course of history. The evolution of AI is not just a technical shift; it is a societal transformation. Throughout history, we have witnessed how revolutions in technology reshape civilization—from the steam engine to the internet. AI follows this trajectory, with the potential to redefine what it means to be human. Every industry, from healthcare to finance, is being disrupted, forcing humanity to adapt in unprecedented ways. The coming decades will determine whether AI remains a tool for prosperity or becomes an uncontrollable force.

AI is expected to continue its exponential growth, leading to exciting yet unpredictable outcomes: AI is not just a technological advancement—it is a revolution redefining humanity's place in the digital age. Its presence is felt in every aspect of life, from the way we work to the way we interact, reshaping the very fabric of society. Understanding AI means understanding the future, and those who harness its potential will shape the course of history. The evolution of AI is not just a technical shift; it is a societal transformation. Throughout history, we have witnessed how revolutions in technology reshape civilization—from the steam engine to the internet. AI follows this trajectory, with the potential to redefine what it means to be human. Every industry, from healthcare to finance, is being disrupted, forcing humanity to adapt in unprecedented ways. The coming decades will determine whether AI remains a tool for prosperity or becomes an uncontrollable force.

- **Artificial General Intelligence (AGI):** Scientists are working towards developing AGI capable of human-like reasoning.
- **Human-AI Collaboration:** Future workplaces may involve seamless AI-human partnerships.
- **Ethical AI Development:** Policymakers and researchers are working to create ethical AI regulations.
- **AI in Scientific Discovery:** AI is accelerating progress in medicine, climate science, and space exploration.
- **AI in Space Exploration:** AI is assisting in planetary research, navigation, and robotic missions. AI is not just a technological advancement—it is a revolution redefining humanity's place in the digital age. Its presence is felt in every aspect of life, from the way we work to the way we interact, reshaping the very fabric of society. Understanding AI means understanding the future, and those who harness its potential will shape the course of history. The evolution of AI is not just a technical shift; it is a societal transformation. Throughout history, we have witnessed how revolutions in technology reshape civilization—from the steam engine to the internet. AI follows this trajectory, with the potential to redefine what it means to be human. Every industry, from healthcare to finance, is being disrupted, forcing humanity to adapt in unprecedented ways. The coming decades will determine whether AI remains a tool for prosperity or becomes an uncontrollable force.

Conclusion AI is not just a technological advancement—it is a revolution redefining humanity's place in the digital age. Its presence is felt in every aspect of life, from the way we work to the way we interact, reshaping the very fabric of society. Understanding AI means understanding the future, and those who harness its potential will shape the course of history. The evolution of AI is not just a technical shift; it is a societal transformation. Throughout history, we have witnessed how revolutions in technology reshape civilization—from the steam engine to the internet. AI follows this trajectory, with the potential to redefine what it means to be human. Every industry, from healthcare to finance, is being disrupted, forcing humanity to adapt in unprecedented ways. The coming decades will determine whether AI remains a tool for prosperity or becomes an uncontrollable force.

AI is not just a tool for efficiency—it is reshaping the way humans interact with technology and information. As AI advances, society must navigate its opportunities and challenges wisely to ensure AI benefits humanity rather than disrupts it. AI is not just a technological advancement— it is a revolution redefining humanity's place in the digital age. Its presence is felt in every aspect of life, from the way we work to the way we interact, reshaping the very fabric of society. Understanding AI means understanding the future, and those who harness its potential will shape the course of history.

--- AI is not just a technological advancement—it is a revolution redefining humanity's place in the digital age. Its presence is felt in every aspect of life, from the way we work to the way we interact, reshaping the very fabric of society. Understanding AI means understanding the future,

and those who harness its potential will shape the course of history. The evolution of AI is not just a technical shift; it is a societal transformation. Throughout history, we have witnessed how revolutions in technology reshape civilization—from the steam engine to the internet. AI follows this trajectory, with the potential to redefine what it means to be human. Every industry, from healthcare to finance, is being disrupted, forcing humanity to adapt in unprecedented ways. The coming decades will determine whether AI remains a tool for prosperity or becomes an uncontrollable force.

CHAPTER 2: THE HISTORY OF AI

The Origins of Artificial Intelligence AI is not just a technological advancement—it is a revolution redefining humanity's place in the digital age. Its presence is felt in every aspect of life, from the way we work to the way we interact, reshaping the very fabric of society. Understanding AI means understanding the future, and those who harness its potential will shape the course of history. The evolution of AI is not just a technical shift; it is a societal transformation. Throughout history, we have witnessed how revolutions in technology reshape civilization—from the steam engine to the internet. AI follows this trajectory, with the potential to redefine what it means to be human. Every industry, from healthcare to finance, is being disrupted, forcing humanity to adapt in unprecedented ways. The coming decades will determine whether AI remains a tool for prosperity or becomes an uncontrollable force.

The concept of Artificial Intelligence dates back to ancient history when humans imagined mechanical beings with human-like intelligence. However, the formal study of AI began in the mid-20th century with advances in computer science and mathematics. Early philosophers, mathematicians, and logicians pondered whether machines could think, setting the stage for AI research. The evolution of AI is not just a technical shift; it is a societal transformation. Throughout history, we have witnessed how revolutions in technology reshape civilization— from the steam engine to the internet. AI follows this trajectory, with the potential to redefine what it means to be human. Every industry, from healthcare to finance, is being disrupted, forcing humanity to adapt in unprecedented ways. The coming decades will determine whether AI remains a tool for prosperity or becomes an uncontrollable force.

The Early Thinkers of AI AI is not just a technological advancement—it is a revolution redefining humanity's place in the digital age. Its presence is felt in every aspect of life, from the way we work to the way we interact, reshaping the very fabric of society. Understanding AI means understanding the future, and those who harness its potential will shape the course of history. The evolution of AI is not just a technical shift; it is a societal transformation. Throughout history, we have witnessed how revolutions in technology reshape civilization—from the steam engine to the internet. AI follows this trajectory, with the potential to redefine what it means to be human. Every industry, from healthcare to finance, is being disrupted, forcing humanity to adapt in unprecedented ways. The coming decades will determine whether AI remains a tool for prosperity or becomes an uncontrollable force.

- **Alan Turing (1950):** Proposed the idea that machines could simulate human intelligence, introducing the famous "Turing Test."
- **John McCarthy (1956):** Coined the term "Artificial Intelligence" at the Dartmouth Conference, marking AI as an academic discipline.
- **Marvin Minsky and Herbert Simon:** Developed some of the first AI programs capable of reasoning and problem-solving. AI is not just a technological advancement—it is a revolution redefining humanity's place in the digital age. Its presence is felt in every aspect of life, from the way we work to the way we interact, reshaping the very fabric of society. Understanding AI means understanding the future, and those who harness its potential will shape the course of history. The evolution of AI is not just a technical shift; it is a societal transformation. Throughout history, we have witnessed how revolutions in technology reshape civilization—from the steam engine to the internet. AI follows this trajectory, with the potential to redefine what it means to be human. Every industry, from healthcare to finance, is being disrupted, forcing humanity to adapt in unprecedented ways. The coming decades will determine whether AI remains a tool for prosperity or becomes an uncontrollable force.

During this period, AI research focused on **symbolic reasoning**, rule-based systems, and formal logic. Scientists believed AI would soon replicate human intelligence, but progress was slower than expected. AI is not just a technological advancement—it is a revolution redefining humanity's place in the digital age. Its presence is felt in every aspect of life, from the way we work to the way we interact, reshaping the very fabric of society. Understanding AI means understanding the future, and those who harness its potential will shape the course of history.

The Birth of AI Research AI is not just a technological advancement—it is a revolution redefining humanity's place in the digital age. Its presence is felt in every aspect of life, from the way we work to the way we interact, reshaping the very fabric of society. Understanding AI means understanding the future, and those who harness its potential will shape the course of history. The evolution of AI is not just a technical shift; it is a societal transformation. Throughout history, we have witnessed how revolutions in technology reshape civilization—from the steam engine to the internet. AI follows this trajectory, with the potential to redefine what it means to be human. Every industry, from healthcare to finance, is being disrupted, forcing humanity to adapt in unprecedented ways. The coming decades will determine whether AI remains a tool for prosperity or becomes an uncontrollable force.

The **1956 Dartmouth Conference** was a turning point, establishing AI as a formal field of study. Key developments in this period included: AI is not just a technological advancement—it is a revolution redefining humanity's place in the digital age. Its presence is felt in every aspect of life, from the way we work to the way we interact, reshaping the very fabric of society. Understanding AI means understanding the future, and those who harness its potential will shape the course of history. The evolution of AI is not just a technical shift; it is a societal transformation. Throughout history, we have witnessed how revolutions in technology reshape civilization—from the steam engine to the internet. AI follows this trajectory, with the potential to redefine what it means to be human. Every industry, from healthcare to finance, is being disrupted, forcing humanity to adapt in unprecedented ways. The coming decades will determine whether AI remains a tool for prosperity or becomes an uncontrollable force.

- **Logic Theorist (1955-1956):** The first AI program that could prove mathematical theorems.
- **ELIZA (1960s):** An early natural language processing chatbot that mimicked human conversation.
- **Expert Systems (1970s):** Programs designed to emulate human decision-making in specialized fields, such as medicine and engineering. AI is not just a technological advancement—it is a revolution redefining humanity's place in the digital age. Its presence is felt in every aspect of life, from the way we work to the way we interact, reshaping the very fabric of society. Understanding AI means understanding the future, and those who harness its potential will shape the course of history. The evolution of AI is not just a technical shift; it is a societal transformation. Throughout history, we have witnessed how revolutions in technology reshape civilization—from the steam engine to the internet. AI follows this trajectory, with the potential to redefine what it means to be human. Every industry, from healthcare to finance, is being disrupted, forcing humanity to adapt in unprecedented ways. The coming decades will determine whether AI remains a tool for prosperity or becomes an uncontrollable force.

The AI Winters: Periods of Decline AI is not just a technological advancement—it is a revolution redefining humanity's place in the digital age. Its presence is felt in every aspect of life, from the way we work to the way we interact, reshaping the very fabric of society. Understanding AI means understanding the future, and those who harness its potential will shape the course of history. The evolution of AI is not just a technical shift; it is a societal transformation. Throughout history, we have witnessed how revolutions in technology reshape civilization—from the steam engine to the internet. AI follows this trajectory, with the potential to redefine what it means to be human. Every industry, from healthcare to finance, is being disrupted, forcing humanity to adapt in unprecedented ways. The coming decades will determine whether AI remains a tool for prosperity or becomes an uncontrollable force.

Despite early optimism, AI research faced major setbacks due to overhyped expectations. Government funding and interest declined, leading to periods known as **AI Winters**: AI is not just a technological advancement—it is a revolution redefining humanity's place in the digital age. Its presence is felt in every aspect of life, from the way we work to the way we interact, reshaping the very fabric of society. Understanding AI means understanding the future, and those who harness its potential will shape the course of history. The evolution of AI is not just a technical shift; it is a societal transformation. Throughout history, we have witnessed how revolutions in technology reshape civilization—from the steam engine to the internet. AI follows this trajectory, with the potential to redefine what it means to be human. Every industry, from healthcare to finance, is being disrupted, forcing humanity to adapt in unprecedented ways. The coming decades will determine whether AI remains a tool for prosperity or becomes an uncontrollable force.

- **First AI Winter (1974-1980s):** Funding dried up due to slow progress and unmet promises. AI systems were not as intelligent as expected.
- **Second AI Winter (1987-1993):** Expert systems, once considered revolutionary, proved costly and impractical. The limitations of symbolic AI became evident. The evolution of AI is not just a technical shift; it is a societal transformation. Throughout history, we have witnessed how revolutions in technology reshape civilization—from the steam engine to the internet. AI follows this trajectory, with the potential to redefine what it means to be human. Every industry, from healthcare to finance, is being disrupted, forcing humanity to adapt in unprecedented ways. The coming decades will determine whether AI remains a tool for prosperity or becomes an uncontrollable force.

These challenges forced researchers to rethink AI's approach, leading to a renewed focus on **machine learning and statistical models** rather than purely symbolic reasoning. AI is not just a technological advancement—it is a revolution redefining humanity's place in the digital age. Its presence is felt in every aspect of life, from the way we work to the way we interact, reshaping the very fabric of society. Understanding AI means understanding the future, and those who harness its potential will shape the course of history. The evolution of AI is not just a technical shift; it is a societal transformation. Throughout history, we have witnessed how revolutions in technology reshape civilization—from the steam engine to the internet. AI follows this trajectory, with the potential to redefine what it means to be human. Every industry, from healthcare to finance, is being disrupted, forcing humanity to adapt in unprecedented ways. The coming decades will determine whether AI remains a tool for prosperity or becomes an uncontrollable force.

The AI Renaissance: Machine Learning and Neural Networks

AI is not just a technological advancement—it is a revolution redefining humanity's place in the digital age. Its presence is felt in every aspect of life, from the way we work to the way we interact, reshaping the very fabric of society. Understanding AI means understanding the future, and those who harness its potential will shape the course of history. The evolution of AI is not just a technical shift; it is a societal transformation. Throughout history, we have witnessed how revolutions in technology reshape civilization—from the steam engine to the internet. AI follows this trajectory, with the potential to redefine what it means to be human. Every industry, from healthcare to finance, is being disrupted, forcing humanity to adapt in unprecedented ways. The coming decades will determine whether AI remains a tool for prosperity or becomes an uncontrollable force.

AI research resurged in the 1990s and 2000s with breakthroughs in **machine learning and neural networks**: AI is not just a technological advancement—it is a revolution redefining humanity's place in the digital age. Its presence is felt in every aspect of life, from the way we work to the way we interact, reshaping the very fabric of society. Understanding AI means understanding the future, and those who harness its potential will shape the course of history. The evolution of AI is not just a technical shift; it is a societal transformation. Throughout history, we have witnessed how revolutions in technology reshape civilization—from the steam engine to the internet. AI follows this trajectory, with the potential to redefine what it means to be human. Every industry, from healthcare to finance, is being disrupted, forcing humanity to adapt in unprecedented ways. The coming decades will determine whether AI remains a tool for prosperity or becomes an uncontrollable force.

- **1997:** IBM's Deep Blue defeats chess world champion Garry Kasparov, showcasing AI's ability to outperform humans in structured decision-making.
- **2011:** IBM Watson wins Jeopardy!, demonstrating AI's potential in natural language processing.
- **2012:** Deep learning revolution begins with AlexNet outperforming human accuracy in image recognition. Neural networks and large datasets enabled AI to learn from experience. AI is not just a technological advancement—it is a revolution redefining humanity's place in the digital age. Its presence is felt in every aspect of life, from the way we work to the way we interact, reshaping the very fabric of society. Understanding AI means understanding the future, and those who harness its potential will shape the course of history.

The Modern AI Boom AI is not just a technological advancement—it is a revolution redefining humanity's place in the digital age. Its presence is felt in every aspect of life, from the way we work to the way we interact, reshaping the very fabric of society. Understanding AI means understanding the future, and those who harness its potential will shape the course of history. The evolution of AI is not just a technical shift; it is a societal transformation. Throughout history, we have witnessed how revolutions in technology reshape civilization—from the steam engine to the internet. AI follows this trajectory, with the potential to redefine what it means to be human. Every industry, from healthcare to finance, is being disrupted, forcing humanity to adapt in unprecedented ways. The coming decades will determine whether AI remains a tool for prosperity or becomes an uncontrollable force.

AI has advanced rapidly in the 21st century, driven by big data, powerful GPUs, and new algorithms: AI is not just a technological advancement—it is a revolution redefining humanity's place in the digital age. Its presence is felt in every aspect of life, from the way we work to the way we interact, reshaping the very fabric of society. Understanding AI means understanding the future, and those who harness its potential will shape the course of history. The evolution of AI is not just a technical shift; it is a societal transformation. Throughout history, we have witnessed how revolutions in technology reshape civilization—from the steam engine to the internet. AI follows this trajectory, with the potential to redefine what it means to be human. Every industry, from healthcare to finance, is being disrupted, forcing humanity to adapt in unprecedented ways. The coming decades will determine whether AI remains a tool for prosperity or becomes an uncontrollable force.

- **2016:** AlphaGo beats human champions in Go, a game previously thought impossible for AI to master.
- **2020s:** AI-powered chatbots, self-driving cars, and generative models (e.g., GPT-4, DALL·E) redefine human-computer interaction.
- **AI in Daily Life:** AI is now integrated into personal assistants, financial trading, healthcare, and creative industries. AI is not just a technological advancement—it is a revolution redefining humanity's place in the digital age. Its presence is felt in every aspect of life, from the way we work to the way we interact, reshaping the very fabric of society. Understanding AI means understanding the future, and those who harness its potential will shape the course of history. The evolution of AI is not just a technical shift; it is a societal transformation. Throughout history, we have witnessed how revolutions in technology reshape civilization—from the steam engine to the internet. AI follows this trajectory, with the potential to redefine what it means to be human. Every industry, from healthcare to finance, is being disrupted, forcing humanity to adapt in unprecedented ways. The coming decades will determine whether AI remains a tool for prosperity or becomes an uncontrollable force.

Ethical Considerations in AI History AI is not just a technological advancement—it is a revolution redefining humanity's place in the digital age. Its presence is felt in every aspect of life, from the way we work to the way we interact, reshaping the very fabric of society. Understanding AI means understanding the future, and those who harness its potential will shape the course of history. The evolution of AI is not just a technical shift; it is a societal transformation. Throughout history, we have witnessed how revolutions in technology reshape civilization—from the steam engine to the internet. AI follows this trajectory, with the potential to redefine what it means to be human. Every industry, from healthcare to finance, is being disrupted, forcing humanity to adapt in unprecedented ways. The coming decades will determine whether AI remains a tool for prosperity or becomes an uncontrollable force.

As AI has evolved, so have ethical debates: AI is not just a technological advancement—it is a revolution redefining humanity's place in the digital age. Its presence is felt in every aspect of life, from the way we work to the way we interact, reshaping the very fabric of society. Understanding AI means understanding the future, and those who harness its potential will shape the course of history. The evolution of AI is not just a technical shift; it is a societal transformation. Throughout history, we have witnessed how revolutions in technology reshape civilization—from the steam engine to the internet. AI follows this trajectory, with the potential to redefine what it means to be human. Every industry, from healthcare to finance, is being disrupted, forcing humanity to adapt in unprecedented ways. The coming decades will determine whether AI remains a tool for prosperity or becomes an uncontrollable force.

- **The Role of Bias:** AI models inherit biases from their training data.
- **Automation and Workforce Displacement:** AI is transforming industries, sometimes replacing human labor.
- **AI in Warfare:** Autonomous weapons and AI-driven cybersecurity raise concerns. AI is not just a technological advancement—it is a revolution redefining humanity's place in the digital age. Its presence is felt in every aspect of life, from the way we work to the way we interact, reshaping the very fabric of society. Understanding AI means understanding the future, and those who harness its potential will shape the course of history. The evolution of AI is not just a technical shift; it is a societal transformation. Throughout history, we have witnessed how revolutions in technology reshape civilization—from the steam engine to the internet. AI follows this trajectory, with the potential to redefine what it means to be human. Every industry, from healthcare to finance, is being disrupted, forcing humanity to adapt in unprecedented ways. The coming decades will determine whether AI remains a tool for prosperity or becomes an uncontrollable force.

The Future: Lessons from AI's Past AI is not just a technological advancement—it is a revolution redefining humanity's place in the digital age. Its presence is felt in every aspect of life, from the way we work to the way we interact, reshaping the very fabric of society. Understanding AI means understanding the future, and those who harness its potential will shape the course of history. The evolution of AI is not just a technical shift; it is a societal transformation. Throughout history, we have witnessed how revolutions in technology reshape civilization—from the steam engine to the internet. AI follows this trajectory, with the potential to redefine what it means to be human. Every industry, from healthcare to finance, is being disrupted, forcing humanity to adapt in unprecedented ways. The coming decades will determine whether AI remains a tool for prosperity or becomes an uncontrollable force.

The history of AI teaches us that progress is not linear. AI research has faced obstacles, but each setback has led to innovation and renewed interest. As AI advances, ethical governance and responsible innovation will determine its long-term impact on society. Understanding AI's past helps us navigate its future wisely. The evolution of AI is not just a technical shift; it is a societal transformation. Throughout history, we have witnessed how revolutions in technology reshape civilization—from the steam engine to the internet. AI follows this trajectory, with the potential to redefine what it means to be human. Every industry, from healthcare to finance, is being disrupted, forcing humanity to adapt in unprecedented ways. The coming decades will determine whether AI remains a tool for prosperity or becomes an uncontrollable force.

--- AI is not just a technological advancement—it is a revolution redefining humanity's place in the digital age. Its presence is felt in every aspect of life, from the way we work to the way we interact, reshaping the very fabric of society. Understanding AI means understanding the future, and those who harness its potential will shape the course of history. The evolution of AI is not just a technical shift; it is a societal transformation. Throughout history, we have witnessed how revolutions in technology reshape civilization—from the steam engine to the internet. AI follows this trajectory, with the potential to redefine what it means to be human. Every industry, from healthcare to finance, is being disrupted, forcing humanity to adapt in unprecedented ways. The coming decades will determine whether AI remains a tool for prosperity or becomes an uncontrollable force.

CHAPTER 3: AI TODAY – WHERE WE STAND

Introduction AI is not just a technological advancement—it is a revolution redefining humanity's place in the digital age. Its presence is felt in every aspect of life, from the way we work to the way we interact, reshaping the very fabric of society. Understanding AI means understanding the future, and those who harness its potential will shape the course of history. The evolution of AI is not just a technical shift; it is a societal transformation. Throughout history, we have witnessed how revolutions in technology reshape civilization—from the steam engine to the internet. AI follows this trajectory, with the potential to redefine what it means to be human. Every industry, from healthcare to finance, is being disrupted, forcing humanity to adapt in unprecedented ways. The coming decades will determine whether AI remains a tool for prosperity or becomes an uncontrollable force.

Artificial Intelligence has rapidly integrated into our daily lives and industries. AI today is no longer just a theoretical concept but a driving force behind business, healthcare, creativity, and governance. The increasing accessibility of AI tools has led to both widespread innovation and critical ethical concerns. The evolution of AI is not just a technical shift; it is a societal transformation. Throughout history, we have witnessed how revolutions in technology reshape civilization—from the steam engine to the internet. AI follows this trajectory, with the potential to redefine what it means to be human. Every industry, from healthcare to finance, is being disrupted, forcing humanity to adapt in unprecedented ways. The coming decades will determine whether AI remains a tool for prosperity or becomes an uncontrollable force.

The Current State of AI AI is not just a technological advancement—it is a revolution redefining humanity's place in the digital age. Its presence is felt in every aspect of life, from the way we work to the way we interact, reshaping the very fabric of society. Understanding AI means understanding the future, and those who harness its potential will shape the course of history. The evolution of AI is not just a technical shift; it is a societal transformation. Throughout history, we have witnessed how revolutions in technology reshape civilization—from the steam engine to the internet. AI follows this trajectory, with the potential to redefine what it means to be human. Every industry, from healthcare to finance, is being disrupted, forcing humanity to adapt in unprecedented ways. The coming decades will determine whether AI remains a tool for prosperity or becomes an uncontrollable force.

AI has evolved beyond simple automation, becoming an integral part of decision-making processes in various sectors. Modern AI relies on deep learning, neural networks, and big data to perform tasks that were once exclusive to human intelligence. AI is not just a technological advancement—it is a revolution redefining humanity's place in the digital age. Its presence is felt in every aspect of life, from the way we work to the way we interact, reshaping the very fabric of society. Understanding AI means understanding the future, and those who harness its potential will shape the course of history.

AI in Business and Industry AI is not just a technological advancement—it is a revolution redefining humanity's place in the

digital age. Its presence is felt in every aspect of life, from the way we work to the way we interact, reshaping the very fabric of society. Understanding AI means understanding the future, and those who harness its potential will shape the course of history. The evolution of AI is not just a technical shift; it is a societal transformation. Throughout history, we have witnessed how revolutions in technology reshape civilization—from the steam engine to the internet. AI follows this trajectory, with the potential to redefine what it means to be human. Every industry, from healthcare to finance, is being disrupted, forcing humanity to adapt in unprecedented ways. The coming decades will determine whether AI remains a tool for prosperity or becomes an uncontrollable force.

- **AI in Automation:** Businesses use AI to optimize workflows, manage supply chains, and enhance productivity. AI-powered robotic process automation (RPA) streamlines repetitive tasks.
- **AI in Customer Service:** AI chatbots handle millions of customer inquiries daily, improving response times and reducing labor costs.
- **AI in Financial Markets:** Algorithmic trading AI systems analyze vast amounts of market data to predict stock movements with high accuracy. AI is not just a technological advancement—it is a revolution redefining humanity's place in the digital age. Its presence is felt in every aspect of life, from the way we work to the way we interact, reshaping the very fabric of society. Understanding AI means understanding the future, and those who harness its potential will shape the course of history.

AI in Healthcare AI is not just a technological advancement—it is a revolution redefining humanity's place in the digital age. Its presence is felt in every aspect of life, from the way we work to the way we interact, reshaping the very fabric of society. Understanding AI means understanding the future, and those who harness its potential will shape the course of history. The evolution of AI is not just a technical shift; it is a societal transformation. Throughout history, we have witnessed how revolutions in technology reshape civilization—from the steam engine to the internet. AI follows this trajectory, with the potential to redefine what it means to be human. Every industry, from

healthcare to finance, is being disrupted, forcing humanity to adapt in unprecedented ways. The coming decades will determine whether AI remains a tool for prosperity or becomes an uncontrollable force.

- **AI-Powered Diagnostics:** AI assists in detecting diseases such as cancer, outperforming human doctors in accuracy.
- **AI in Drug Discovery:** AI shortens the time required for developing new medications by simulating chemical interactions.
- **AI and Telemedicine:** AI-driven healthcare assistants provide preliminary diagnoses, making medical expertise accessible remotely. AI is not just a technological advancement—it is a revolution redefining humanity's place in the digital age. Its presence is felt in every aspect of life, from the way we work to the way we interact, reshaping the very fabric of society. Understanding AI means understanding the future, and those who harness its potential will shape the course of history. The evolution of AI is not just a technical shift; it is a societal transformation. Throughout history, we have witnessed how revolutions in technology reshape civilization—from the steam engine to the internet. AI follows this trajectory, with the potential to redefine what it means to be human. Every industry, from healthcare to finance, is being disrupted, forcing humanity to adapt in unprecedented ways. The coming decades will determine whether AI remains a tool for prosperity or becomes an uncontrollable force.

AI in Creativity and Content Generation AI is not just a technological advancement—it is a revolution redefining humanity's place in the digital age. Its presence is felt in every aspect of life, from the way we work to the way we interact, reshaping the very fabric of society. Understanding AI means understanding the future, and those who harness its potential will shape the course of history. The evolution of AI is not just a technical shift; it is a societal transformation. Throughout history, we have witnessed how revolutions in technology reshape civilization—from the steam engine to the internet. AI follows this trajectory, with the potential to redefine what it means to be human. Every industry, from healthcare to finance, is being disrupted, forcing humanity to adapt in unprecedented ways. The coming decades will determine whether AI remains a tool for prosperity or becomes an uncontrollable force.

AI is making an impact in creative industries, reshaping how content is produced. AI is not just a technological advancement—it is a revolution redefining humanity's place in the digital age. Its presence is felt in every aspect of life, from the way we work to the way we interact, reshaping the very fabric of society. Understanding AI means understanding the future, and those who harness its potential will shape the course of history. The evolution of AI is not just a technical shift; it is a societal transformation. Throughout history, we have witnessed how revolutions in technology reshape civilization—from the steam engine to the internet. AI follows this trajectory, with the potential to redefine what it means to be human. Every industry, from healthcare to finance, is being disrupted, forcing humanity to adapt in unprecedented ways. The coming decades will determine whether AI remains a tool for prosperity or becomes an uncontrollable force.

- **AI-Generated Art and Music:** AI models like DALL·E and Amper create original paintings and compositions.
- **AI in Writing:** AI-powered tools assist authors, journalists, and content creators, generating articles and scripts.
- **AI in Film and Media:** AI-enhanced CGI, deepfake technology, and AI-driven scriptwriting are revolutionizing entertainment. AI is not just a technological advancement—it is a revolution redefining humanity's place in the digital age. Its presence is felt in every aspect of life, from the way we work to the way we interact, reshaping the very fabric of society. Understanding AI means understanding the future, and those who harness its potential will shape the course of history. The evolution of AI is not just a technical shift; it is a societal transformation. Throughout history, we have witnessed how revolutions in technology reshape civilization—from the steam engine to the internet. AI follows this trajectory, with the potential to redefine what it means to be human. Every industry, from healthcare to finance, is being disrupted, forcing humanity to adapt in unprecedented ways. The coming decades will determine whether AI remains a tool for prosperity or becomes an uncontrollable force.

The Ethical Dilemmas of AI AI is not just a technological advancement—it is a revolution redefining humanity's place in the digital age. Its presence is felt in every aspect of life, from the way we work to the way we interact, reshaping the very fabric of society. Understanding AI means understanding the future, and those who harness its potential will shape the course of history. The evolution of AI is not just a technical shift; it is a societal transformation. Throughout history, we have witnessed how revolutions in technology reshape civilization—from the steam engine to the internet. AI follows this trajectory, with the potential to redefine what it means to be human. Every industry, from healthcare to finance, is being disrupted, forcing humanity to adapt in unprecedented ways. The coming decades will determine whether AI remains a tool for prosperity or becomes an uncontrollable force.

As AI permeates society, it brings ethical concerns that need urgent attention. AI is not just a technological advancement—it is a revolution redefining humanity's place in the digital age. Its presence is felt in every aspect of life, from the way we work to the way we interact, reshaping the very fabric of society. Understanding AI means understanding the future, and those who harness its potential will shape the course of history. The evolution of AI is not just a technical shift; it is a societal transformation. Throughout history, we have witnessed how revolutions in technology reshape civilization—from the steam engine to the internet. AI follows this trajectory, with the potential to redefine what it means to be human. Every industry, from healthcare to finance, is being disrupted, forcing humanity to adapt in unprecedented ways. The coming decades will determine whether AI remains a tool for prosperity or becomes an uncontrollable force.

AI and Bias AI is not just a technological advancement—it is a revolution redefining humanity's place in the digital age. Its presence is felt in every aspect of life, from the way we work to the way we interact, reshaping the very fabric of society. Understanding AI means understanding the future, and those who harness its potential will shape the course of history. The evolution of AI is not just a technical shift; it is a societal transformation. Throughout history, we have witnessed how revolutions in technology reshape civilization—from the steam engine to the internet. AI follows this trajectory, with the potential to redefine what it means to be human. Every industry, from healthcare to finance, is being disrupted, forcing humanity to adapt in unprecedented ways. The coming decades will determine whether AI remains a tool for prosperity or becomes an uncontrollable force.

- **Bias in Hiring Algorithms:** AI-driven hiring tools have shown bias against minority candidates due to skewed training data.
- **AI in Criminal Justice:** AI-powered crime prediction models raise concerns about racial profiling and discrimination. AI is not just a technological advancement—it is a revolution redefining humanity's place in the digital age. Its presence is felt in every aspect of life, from the way we work to the way we interact, reshaping the very fabric of society. Understanding AI means understanding the future, and those who harness its potential will shape the course of history. The evolution of AI is not just a technical shift; it is a societal transformation. Throughout history, we have witnessed how revolutions in technology reshape civilization—from the steam engine to the internet. AI follows this trajectory, with the potential to redefine what it means to be human. Every industry, from healthcare to finance, is being disrupted, forcing humanity to adapt in unprecedented ways. The coming decades will determine whether AI remains a tool for prosperity or becomes an uncontrollable force.

Privacy and AI Surveillance AI is not just a technological advancement—it is a revolution redefining humanity's place in the digital age. Its presence is felt in every aspect of life, from the way we work to the way we interact, reshaping the very fabric of society. Understanding AI means understanding the future, and those who harness its potential will shape the course of history. The evolution of AI is not just a technical shift; it is a societal transformation.

Throughout history, we have witnessed how revolutions in technology reshape civilization—from the steam engine to the internet. AI follows this trajectory, with the potential to redefine what it means to be human. Every industry, from healthcare to finance, is being disrupted, forcing humanity to adapt in unprecedented ways. The coming decades will determine whether AI remains a tool for prosperity or becomes an uncontrollable force.

- **Facial Recognition Technology:** AI-powered surveillance systems raise concerns about mass surveillance and personal freedoms.
- **AI and Data Security:** AI's ability to track and analyze online behavior sparks debates about personal privacy. AI is not just a technological advancement—it is a revolution redefining humanity's place in the digital age. Its presence is felt in every aspect of life, from the way we work to the way we interact, reshaping the very fabric of society. Understanding AI means understanding the future, and those who harness its potential will shape the course of history. The evolution of AI is not just a technical shift; it is a societal transformation. Throughout history, we have witnessed how revolutions in technology reshape civilization—from the steam engine to the internet. AI follows this trajectory, with the potential to redefine what it means to be human. Every industry, from healthcare to finance, is being disrupted, forcing humanity to adapt in unprecedented ways. The coming decades will determine whether AI remains a tool for prosperity or becomes an uncontrollable force.

AI and Workforce Displacement AI is not just a technological advancement—it is a revolution redefining humanity's place in the digital age. Its presence is felt in every aspect of life, from the way we work to the way we interact, reshaping the very fabric of society. Understanding AI means understanding the future, and those who harness its potential will shape the course of history. The evolution of AI is not just a technical shift; it is a societal transformation. Throughout history, we have witnessed how revolutions in technology reshape civilization—from the steam engine to the internet. AI follows this trajectory, with the potential to redefine what it means to be human. Every industry, from healthcare to finance, is being disrupted, forcing humanity to adapt in unprecedented ways. The coming

decades will determine whether AI remains a tool for prosperity or becomes an uncontrollable force.

- **Automation and Job Losses:** AI is replacing traditional jobs in industries like manufacturing, customer service, and retail.
- **The Future of Employment:** While some jobs are lost, new AI-related careers such as AI ethics specialists and machine learning engineers are emerging. AI is not just a technological advancement—it is a revolution redefining humanity's place in the digital age. Its presence is felt in every aspect of life, from the way we work to the way we interact, reshaping the very fabric of society. Understanding AI means understanding the future, and those who harness its potential will shape the course of history. The evolution of AI is not just a technical shift; it is a societal transformation. Throughout history, we have witnessed how revolutions in technology reshape civilization—from the steam engine to the internet. AI follows this trajectory, with the potential to redefine what it means to be human. Every industry, from healthcare to finance, is being disrupted, forcing humanity to adapt in unprecedented ways. The coming decades will determine whether AI remains a tool for prosperity or becomes an uncontrollable force.

The Risks and Rewards of AI Today AI is not just a technological advancement—it is a revolution redefining humanity's place in the digital age. Its presence is felt in every aspect of life, from the way we work to the way we interact, reshaping the very fabric of society. Understanding AI means understanding the future, and those who harness its potential will shape the course of history. The evolution of AI is not just a technical shift; it is a societal transformation. Throughout history, we have witnessed how revolutions in technology reshape civilization—from the steam engine to the internet. AI follows this trajectory, with the potential to redefine what it means to be human. Every industry, from healthcare to finance, is being disrupted, forcing humanity to adapt in unprecedented ways. The coming decades will determine whether AI remains a tool for prosperity or becomes an uncontrollable force.

While AI presents incredible opportunities, it also carries risks. AI is not just a technological advancement—it is a revolution redefining humanity's place in the digital age. Its presence is felt in every aspect of life, from the way we work to the way we interact, reshaping the very fabric of society. Understanding AI means understanding the future, and those who harness its potential will shape the course of history. The evolution of AI is not just a technical shift; it is a societal transformation. Throughout history, we have witnessed how revolutions in technology reshape civilization—from the steam engine to the internet. AI follows this trajectory, with the potential to redefine what it means to be human. Every industry, from healthcare to finance, is being disrupted, forcing humanity to adapt in unprecedented ways. The coming decades will determine whether AI remains a tool for prosperity or becomes an uncontrollable force.

- **AI in Misinformation:** Deepfakes and AI-generated fake news threaten trust in online content.
- **The Fear of AI Autonomy:** Some experts worry about AI systems making independent decisions without human oversight. AI is not just a technological advancement—it is a revolution redefining humanity's place in the digital age. Its presence is felt in every aspect of life, from the way we work to the way we interact, reshaping the very fabric of society. Understanding AI means understanding the future, and those who harness its potential will shape the course of history. The evolution of AI is not just a technical shift; it is a societal transformation. Throughout history, we have witnessed how revolutions in technology reshape civilization—from the steam engine to the internet. AI follows this trajectory, with the potential to redefine what it means to be human. Every industry, from healthcare to finance, is being disrupted, forcing humanity to adapt in unprecedented ways. The coming decades will determine whether AI remains a tool for prosperity or becomes an uncontrollable force.

Conclusion AI is not just a technological advancement—it is a revolution redefining humanity's place in the digital age. Its presence is felt in every aspect of life, from the way we work to the way we interact, reshaping the very fabric of society. Understanding AI means understanding the future, and those who harness its potential will shape the course of history. The evolution of AI is not just a technical shift; it is a societal transformation. Throughout history, we have witnessed how revolutions in technology reshape civilization—from the steam engine to the internet. AI follows this trajectory, with the potential to redefine what it means to be human. Every industry, from healthcare to finance, is being disrupted, forcing humanity to adapt in unprecedented ways. The coming decades will determine whether AI remains a tool for prosperity or becomes an uncontrollable force.

AI is at the center of technological progress, but its trajectory depends on responsible development and regulation. Understanding AI's strengths and weaknesses will help shape a future where AI benefits humanity while mitigating risks. AI is not just a technological advancement—it is a revolution redefining humanity's place in the digital age. Its presence is felt in every aspect of life, from the way we work to the way we interact, reshaping the very fabric of society. Understanding AI means understanding the future, and those who harness its potential will shape the course of history.

--- AI is not just a technological advancement—it is a revolution redefining humanity's place in the digital age. Its presence is felt in every aspect of life, from the way we work to the way we interact, reshaping the very fabric of society. Understanding AI means understanding the future,

and those who harness its potential will shape the course of history. The evolution of AI is not just a technical shift; it is a societal transformation. Throughout history, we have witnessed how revolutions in technology reshape civilization—from the steam engine to the internet. AI follows this trajectory, with the potential to redefine what it means to be human. Every industry, from healthcare to finance, is being disrupted, forcing humanity to adapt in unprecedented ways. The coming decades will determine whether AI remains a tool for prosperity or becomes an uncontrollable force.

CHAPTER 4: MAKING MONEY WITH AI

Introduction AI is not just a technological advancement—it is a revolution redefining humanity's place in the digital age. Its presence is felt in every aspect of life, from the way we work to the way we interact, reshaping the very fabric of society. Understanding AI means understanding the future, and those who harness its potential will shape the course of history. The evolution of AI is not just a technical shift; it is a societal transformation. Throughout history, we have witnessed how revolutions in technology reshape civilization—from the steam engine to the internet. AI follows this trajectory, with the potential to redefine what it means to be human. Every industry, from healthcare to finance, is being disrupted, forcing humanity to adapt in unprecedented ways. The coming decades will determine whether AI remains a tool for prosperity or becomes an uncontrollable force.

Artificial Intelligence is not just transforming industries; it is creating new financial opportunities for individuals and businesses. Whether through automation, investment, or AI-driven entrepreneurship, AI is unlocking pathways to wealth creation. This chapter explores how AI can be leveraged for financial gain in various sectors. The evolution of AI is not just a technical shift; it is a societal transformation. Throughout history, we have witnessed how revolutions in technology reshape civilization—from the steam engine to the internet. AI follows this trajectory, with the potential to redefine what it means to be human. Every industry, from healthcare to finance, is being disrupted, forcing humanity to adapt in unprecedented ways. The coming decades will determine whether AI remains a tool for prosperity or becomes an uncontrollable force.

AI-Powered Business Models AI is not just a technological advancement—it is a revolution redefining humanity's place in the digital age. Its presence is felt in every aspect of life, from the way we work to the way we interact, reshaping the very fabric of society. Understanding AI means understanding the future, and those who harness its potential will shape the course of history. The evolution of AI is not just a technical shift; it is a societal transformation. Throughout history, we have witnessed how revolutions in technology reshape civilization—from the steam engine to the internet. AI follows this trajectory, with the potential to redefine what it means to be human. Every industry, from healthcare to finance, is being disrupted, forcing humanity to adapt in unprecedented ways. The coming decades will determine whether AI remains a tool for prosperity or becomes an uncontrollable force.

AI is enabling new business models that leverage automation, personalization, and data-driven decision-making. AI is not just a technological advancement—it is a revolution redefining humanity's place in the digital age. Its presence is felt in every aspect of life, from the way we work to the way we interact, reshaping the very fabric of society. Understanding AI means understanding the future, and those who harness its potential will shape the course of history. The evolution of AI is not just a technical shift; it is a societal transformation. Throughout history, we have witnessed how revolutions in technology reshape civilization—from the steam engine to the internet. AI follows this trajectory, with the potential to redefine what it means to be human. Every industry, from healthcare to finance, is being disrupted, forcing humanity to adapt in unprecedented ways. The coming decades will determine whether AI remains a tool for prosperity or becomes an uncontrollable force.

AI in E-Commerce and Retail AI is not just a technological advancement—it is a revolution redefining humanity's place in the digital age. Its presence is felt in every aspect of life, from the way we work to the way we interact, reshaping the very fabric of society. Understanding AI means understanding the future, and those who harness its potential will shape the course of history. The evolution of AI is not just a technical shift; it is a societal transformation. Throughout history, we have witnessed how revolutions in technology reshape civilization—from the steam engine to the internet. AI follows this trajectory, with the potential to redefine what it means to be human. Every industry, from healthcare to finance, is being disrupted, forcing humanity to adapt in unprecedented ways. The coming decades will determine whether AI remains a tool for prosperity or becomes an uncontrollable force.

- **AI-Driven Product Recommendations:** AI predicts consumer behavior to personalize shopping experiences and increase sales.
- **AI in Inventory Management:** AI optimizes stock levels, reducing waste and maximizing efficiency.
- **AI Chatbots in Customer Support:** Automated AI-driven chatbots provide 24/7 customer service, reducing costs and improving engagement. AI is not just a technological advancement—it is a revolution redefining humanity's place in the digital age. Its presence is felt in every aspect of life, from the way we work to the way we interact, reshaping the very fabric of society. Understanding AI means understanding the future, and those who harness its potential will shape the course of history. The evolution of AI is not just a technical shift; it is a societal transformation. Throughout history, we have witnessed how revolutions in technology reshape civilization—from the steam engine to the internet. AI follows this trajectory, with the potential to redefine what it means to be human. Every industry, from healthcare to finance, is being disrupted, forcing humanity to adapt in unprecedented ways. The coming decades will determine whether AI remains a tool for prosperity or becomes an uncontrollable force.

AI in Financial Services AI is not just a technological advancement—it is a revolution redefining humanity's place in the digital age. Its presence is felt in every aspect of life, from the way we work to the way we interact, reshaping the very fabric of society. Understanding AI means understanding the future, and those who harness its

potential will shape the course of history. **The evolution of AI is not just a technical shift; it is a societal transformation. Throughout history, we have witnessed how revolutions in technology reshape civilization—from the steam engine to the internet. AI follows this trajectory, with the potential to redefine what it means to be human. Every industry, from healthcare to finance, is being disrupted, forcing humanity to adapt in unprecedented ways. The coming decades will determine whether AI remains a tool for prosperity or becomes an uncontrollable force.**

- **Algorithmic Trading:** AI-powered trading bots analyze market trends and execute trades at high speeds.
- **AI in Fraud Detection:** AI detects suspicious financial transactions and prevents fraud in real-time.
- **AI in Banking:** AI optimizes loan approvals, credit scoring, and personalized financial planning. AI is not just a technological advancement—it is a revolution redefining humanity's place in the digital age. Its presence is felt in every aspect of life, from the way we work to the way we interact, reshaping the very fabric of society. Understanding AI means understanding the future, and those who harness its potential will shape the course of history. The evolution of AI is not just a technical shift; it is a societal transformation. Throughout history, we have witnessed how revolutions in technology reshape civilization—from the steam engine to the internet. AI follows this trajectory, with the potential to redefine what it means to be human. Every industry, from healthcare to finance, is being disrupted, forcing humanity to adapt in unprecedented ways. The coming decades will determine whether AI remains a tool for prosperity or becomes an uncontrollable force.

AI in Content Creation and Digital Marketing AI is not just a technological advancement—it is a revolution redefining humanity's place in the digital age. Its presence is felt in every aspect of life, from the way we work to the way we interact, reshaping the very fabric of society. Understanding AI means understanding the future, and those who harness its potential will shape the course of history. The evolution of AI is not just a technical shift; it is a societal transformation. Throughout history, we have witnessed how revolutions in technology reshape civilization—from the steam engine to the internet. AI follows this trajectory, with the potential to redefine

what it means to be human. Every industry, from healthcare to finance, is being disrupted, forcing humanity to adapt in unprecedented ways. The coming decades will determine whether AI remains a tool for prosperity or becomes an uncontrollable force.

- **AI-Generated Blog Writing:** AI tools automate content creation for websites and businesses, improving SEO rankings.
- **AI in Social Media Management:** AI optimizes posting schedules, engagement strategies, and ad campaigns.
- **AI in Video and Podcast Creation:** AI-generated voiceovers, video editing, and script writing are revolutionizing content production. AI is not just a technological advancement—it is a revolution redefining humanity's place in the digital age. Its presence is felt in every aspect of life, from the way we work to the way we interact, reshaping the very fabric of society. Understanding AI means understanding the future, and those who harness its potential will shape the course of history. The evolution of AI is not just a technical shift; it is a societal transformation. Throughout history, we have witnessed how revolutions in technology reshape civilization—from the steam engine to the internet. AI follows this trajectory, with the potential to redefine what it means to be human. Every industry, from healthcare to finance, is being disrupted, forcing humanity to adapt in unprecedented ways. The coming decades will determine whether AI remains a tool for prosperity or becomes an uncontrollable force.

Making Passive Income with AI AI is not just a technological advancement—it is a revolution redefining humanity's place in the digital age. Its presence is felt in every aspect of life, from the way we work to the way we interact, reshaping the very fabric of society. Understanding AI means understanding the future, and those who harness its potential will shape the course of history. The evolution of AI is not just a technical shift; it is a societal transformation. Throughout history, we have witnessed how revolutions in technology reshape civilization—from the steam engine to the internet. AI follows this trajectory, with the potential to redefine what it means to be human. Every industry, from healthcare to finance, is being disrupted, forcing humanity to adapt in unprecedented ways. The coming decades will determine whether AI remains a tool for prosperity or becomes an uncontrollable force.

AI can generate passive income by automating revenue-generating processes. AI is not just a technological advancement—it is a revolution redefining humanity's place in the digital age. Its presence is felt in every aspect of life, from the way we work to the way we interact, reshaping the very fabric of society. Understanding AI means understanding the future, and those who harness its potential will shape the course of history. The evolution of AI is not just a technical shift; it is a societal transformation. Throughout history, we have witnessed how revolutions in technology reshape civilization—from the steam engine to the internet. AI follows this trajectory, with the potential to redefine what it means to be human. Every industry, from healthcare to finance, is being disrupted, forcing humanity to adapt in unprecedented ways. The coming decades will determine whether AI remains a tool for prosperity or becomes an uncontrollable force.

AI-Driven Automated Businesses AI is not just a technological advancement—it is a revolution redefining humanity's place in the digital age. Its presence is felt in every aspect of life, from the way we work to the way we interact, reshaping the very fabric of society. Understanding AI means understanding the future, and those who harness its potential will shape the course of history. The evolution of AI is not just a technical shift; it is a societal transformation. Throughout history, we have witnessed how revolutions in technology reshape civilization—from the steam engine to the internet. AI follows this trajectory, with the potential to redefine what it means to be human. Every industry, from healthcare to finance, is being disrupted, forcing humanity to adapt in unprecedented ways. The coming decades will determine whether AI remains a tool for prosperity or becomes an uncontrollable force.

- **AI-Powered Subscription Services:** AI-driven SaaS (Software as a Service) tools offer automated services for businesses.
- **AI-Generated Digital Products:** AI creates e-books, stock photos, and online courses for sale. AI is not just a technological advancement—it is a revolution redefining humanity's place in the digital age. Its presence is felt in every aspect of life, from the way we work to the way we interact, reshaping the very fabric of society. Understanding AI means understanding the future, and those who harness its potential will shape the course of history. The evolution of AI is not just a technical shift; it is a societal transformation. Throughout history, we have witnessed how revolutions in technology reshape civilization—from the steam engine to the internet. AI follows this trajectory, with the potential to redefine what it means to be human. Every industry, from healthcare to finance, is being disrupted, forcing humanity to adapt in unprecedented ways. The coming decades will determine whether AI remains a tool for prosperity or becomes an uncontrollable force.

AI in Print-on-Demand and E-Commerce AI is not just a technological advancement—it is a revolution redefining humanity's place in the digital age. Its presence is felt in every aspect of life, from the way we work to the way we interact, reshaping the very fabric of society. Understanding AI means understanding the future, and those who harness its potential will shape the course of history. The

evolution of AI is not just a technical shift; it is a societal transformation. Throughout history, we have witnessed how revolutions in technology reshape civilization—from the steam engine to the internet. AI follows this trajectory, with the potential to redefine what it means to be human. Every industry, from healthcare to finance, is being disrupted, forcing humanity to adapt in unprecedented ways. The coming decades will determine whether AI remains a tool for prosperity or becomes an uncontrollable force.

- **AI-Generated Art and Merchandise:** AI designs graphics for print-on-demand businesses.
- **AI-Powered Dropshipping:** AI automates store management, order fulfillment, and customer support. AI is not just a technological advancement—it is a revolution redefining humanity's place in the digital age. Its presence is felt in every aspect of life, from the way we work to the way we interact, reshaping the very fabric of society. Understanding AI means understanding the future, and those who harness its potential will shape the course of history. The evolution of AI is not just a technical shift; it is a societal transformation. Throughout history, we have witnessed how revolutions in technology reshape civilization—from the steam engine to the internet. AI follows this trajectory, with the potential to redefine what it means to be human. Every industry, from healthcare to finance, is being disrupted, forcing humanity to adapt in unprecedented ways. The coming decades will determine whether AI remains a tool for prosperity or becomes an uncontrollable force.

Investing in AI: The Financial Future AI is not just a technological advancement—it is a revolution redefining humanity's place in the digital age. Its presence is felt in every aspect of life, from the way we work to the way we interact, reshaping the very fabric of society. Understanding AI means understanding the future, and those who harness its potential will shape the course of history. The evolution of AI is not just a technical shift; it is a societal transformation. Throughout history, we have witnessed how revolutions in technology reshape civilization—from the steam engine to the internet. AI follows this trajectory, with the potential to redefine what it means to be human. Every industry, from healthcare to finance, is being disrupted, forcing humanity to adapt in unprecedented ways. The coming decades will determine whether AI remains a tool for prosperity or becomes an uncontrollable force.

AI is reshaping investment strategies, providing new avenues for wealth accumulation. AI is not just a technological advancement—it is a revolution redefining humanity's place in the digital age. Its presence is felt in every aspect of life, from the way we work to the way we interact, reshaping the very fabric of society. Understanding AI means understanding the future, and those who harness its potential will shape the course of history. The evolution of AI is not just a technical shift; it is a societal transformation. Throughout history, we have witnessed how revolutions in technology reshape civilization—from the steam engine to the internet. AI follows this trajectory, with the potential to redefine what it means to be human. Every industry, from healthcare to finance, is being disrupted, forcing humanity to adapt in unprecedented ways. The coming decades will determine whether AI remains a tool for prosperity or becomes an uncontrollable force.

AI in Stock Market Analysis AI is not just a technological advancement—it is a revolution redefining humanity's place in the digital age. Its presence is felt in every aspect of life, from the way we work to the way we interact, reshaping the very fabric of society. Understanding AI means understanding the future, and those who harness its potential will shape the course of history. The evolution of AI is not just a technical shift; it is a societal transformation. Throughout history, we have witnessed how revolutions in technology reshape civilization—from the steam engine to the internet. AI follows this trajectory, with the potential to redefine what it means to be human. Every industry, from healthcare to finance, is being disrupted, forcing humanity to adapt in unprecedented ways. The coming decades will determine whether AI remains a tool for prosperity or becomes an uncontrollable force.

- **Predictive Analytics in Trading:** AI models forecast stock movements based on historical data.
- **Sentiment Analysis for Market Trends:** AI scans news and social media to assess stock sentiment. AI is not just a technological advancement—it is a revolution redefining humanity's place in the digital age. Its presence is felt in every aspect of life, from the way we work to the way we interact, reshaping the very fabric of society. Understanding AI means understanding the future, and those who harness its potential will shape the course of history. The evolution of AI is not just a technical shift; it is a societal transformation. Throughout history, we have witnessed how revolutions in technology reshape civilization—from the steam engine to the internet. AI follows this trajectory, with the potential to redefine what it means to be human. Every industry, from healthcare to finance, is being disrupted, forcing humanity to adapt in unprecedented ways. The coming decades will determine whether AI remains a tool for prosperity or becomes an uncontrollable force.

AI in Cryptocurrency and DeFi (Decentralized Finance) AI is not just a technological advancement—it is a revolution redefining humanity's place in the digital age. Its presence is felt in every aspect of life, from the way we work to the way we interact, reshaping the very fabric of society. Understanding AI means understanding the future, and those who harness its potential will shape the course of history. The

evolution of AI is not just a technical shift; it is a societal transformation. Throughout history, we have witnessed how revolutions in technology reshape civilization—from the steam engine to the internet. AI follows this trajectory, with the potential to redefine what it means to be human. Every industry, from healthcare to finance, is being disrupted, forcing humanity to adapt in unprecedented ways. The coming decades will determine whether AI remains a tool for prosperity or becomes an uncontrollable force.

- **AI-Powered Crypto Trading Bots:** AI predicts price fluctuations and executes trades automatically.
- **AI in Smart Contracts:** AI optimizes decentralized transactions for efficiency and security. AI is not just a technological advancement—it is a revolution redefining humanity's place in the digital age. Its presence is felt in every aspect of life, from the way we work to the way we interact, reshaping the very fabric of society. Understanding AI means understanding the future, and those who harness its potential will shape the course of history. The evolution of AI is not just a technical shift; it is a societal transformation. Throughout history, we have witnessed how revolutions in technology reshape civilization—from the steam engine to the internet. AI follows this trajectory, with the potential to redefine what it means to be human. Every industry, from healthcare to finance, is being disrupted, forcing humanity to adapt in unprecedented ways. The coming decades will determine whether AI remains a tool for prosperity or becomes an uncontrollable force.

The Challenges of AI in Wealth Generation AI is not just a technological advancement—it is a revolution redefining humanity's place in the digital age. Its presence is felt in every aspect of life, from the way we work to the way we interact, reshaping the very fabric of society. Understanding AI means understanding the future, and those who harness its potential will shape the course of history. The evolution of AI is not just a technical shift; it is a societal transformation. Throughout history, we have witnessed how revolutions in technology reshape civilization—from the steam engine to the internet. AI follows this trajectory, with the potential to redefine what it means to be human. Every industry, from healthcare to finance, is being disrupted, forcing humanity to adapt in unprecedented ways. The coming decades will determine whether AI remains a tool for prosperity or becomes an uncontrollable force.

While AI presents financial opportunities, it also comes with challenges: AI is not just a technological advancement—it is a revolution redefining humanity's place in the digital age. Its presence is felt in every aspect of life, from the way we work to the way we interact, reshaping the very fabric of society. Understanding AI means understanding the future, and those who harness its potential will shape the course of history. The evolution of AI is not just a technical shift; it is a societal transformation. Throughout history, we have witnessed how revolutions in technology reshape civilization—from the steam engine to the internet. AI follows this trajectory, with the potential to redefine what it means to be human. Every industry, from healthcare to finance, is being disrupted, forcing humanity to adapt in unprecedented ways. The coming decades will determine whether AI remains a tool for prosperity or becomes an uncontrollable force.

- **AI and Market Volatility:** AI-driven trading increases market unpredictability.
- **Regulatory Concerns:** Governments are developing AI-specific financial regulations to prevent abuse.
- **Job Displacement vs. Job Creation:** AI automation could disrupt traditional industries, requiring new skill sets. AI is not just a technological advancement—it is a revolution redefining humanity's place in the digital age. Its presence is felt in every aspect of life, from the way we work to the way we interact, reshaping the very fabric of society. Understanding AI means understanding the future, and those who harness its potential will shape the course of history.

Conclusion AI is not just a technological advancement—it is a revolution redefining humanity's place in the digital age. Its presence is felt in every aspect of life, from the way we work to the way we interact, reshaping the very fabric of society. Understanding AI means understanding the future, and those who harness its potential will shape the course of history. The evolution of AI is not just a technical shift; it is a societal transformation. Throughout history, we have witnessed how revolutions in technology reshape civilization—from the steam engine to the internet. AI follows this trajectory, with the potential to redefine what it means to be human. Every industry, from healthcare to finance, is being disrupted, forcing humanity to adapt in unprecedented ways. The coming decades will determine whether AI remains a tool for prosperity or becomes an uncontrollable force.

AI is not just changing how we work—it is redefining how we build wealth. Those who embrace AI-driven business models, investments, and automation will be best positioned for the economic future. AI is not just a technological advancement—it is a revolution redefining humanity's place in the digital age. Its presence is felt in every aspect of life, from the way we work to the way we interact, reshaping the very fabric of society. Understanding AI means understanding the future, and those who harness its potential will shape the course of history.

--- AI is not just a technological advancement—it is a revolution redefining humanity's place in the digital age. Its presence is felt in every aspect of life, from the way we work to the way we interact, reshaping the very fabric of society. Understanding AI means understanding the future, and those who harness its potential will shape the course of history. The evolution of AI is not just a technical shift; it is a societal transformation. Throughout history, we have witnessed how revolutions in technology reshape civilization—from the steam engine to the internet. AI follows this trajectory, with the potential to redefine what it means to be human. Every industry, from healthcare to finance, is being disrupted, forcing humanity to adapt in unprecedented ways. The coming decades will determine whether AI remains a tool for prosperity or becomes an uncontrollable force.

CHAPTER 5: AI AND THE HUMAN MIND

Introduction AI is not just a technological advancement—it is a revolution redefining humanity's place in the digital age. Its presence is felt in every aspect of life, from the way we work to the way we interact, reshaping the very fabric of society. Understanding AI means understanding the future, and those who harness its potential will shape the course of history. The evolution of AI is not just a technical shift; it is a societal transformation. Throughout history, we have witnessed how revolutions in technology reshape civilization—from the steam engine to the internet. AI follows this trajectory, with the potential to redefine what it means to be human. Every industry, from healthcare to finance, is being disrupted, forcing humanity to adapt in unprecedented ways. The coming decades will determine whether AI remains a tool for prosperity or becomes an uncontrollable force.

Artificial Intelligence is not just reshaping industries; it is also challenging our understanding of intelligence, creativity, and consciousness. As AI systems become more advanced, questions arise about how they compare to the human mind. AI is not just a technological advancement—it is a revolution redefining humanity's place in the digital age. Its presence is felt in every aspect of life, from the way we work to the way we interact, reshaping the very fabric of society.

Understanding AI means understanding the future, and those who harness its potential will shape the course of history.

AI and Human Cognition AI is not just a technological advancement—it is a revolution redefining humanity's place in the digital age. Its presence is felt in every aspect of life, from the way we work to the way we interact, reshaping the very fabric of society. Understanding AI means understanding the future, and those who harness its potential will shape the course of history. The evolution of AI is not just a technical shift; it is a societal transformation. Throughout history, we have witnessed how revolutions in technology reshape civilization—from the steam engine to the internet. AI follows this trajectory, with the potential to redefine what it means to be human. Every industry, from healthcare to finance, is being disrupted, forcing humanity to adapt in unprecedented ways. The coming decades will determine whether AI remains a tool for prosperity or becomes an uncontrollable force.

AI mimics aspects of human cognition, but fundamental differences remain. AI is not just a technological advancement—it is a revolution redefining humanity's place in the digital age. Its presence is felt in every aspect of life, from the way we work to the way we interact, reshaping the very fabric of society. Understanding AI means understanding the future, and those who harness its potential will shape the course of history. The evolution of AI is not just a technical shift; it is a societal transformation. Throughout history, we have witnessed how revolutions in technology reshape civilization—from the steam engine to the internet. AI follows this trajectory, with the potential to redefine what it means to be human. Every industry, from healthcare to finance, is being disrupted, forcing humanity to adapt in unprecedented ways. The coming decades will determine whether AI remains a tool for prosperity or becomes an uncontrollable force.

- **AI in Pattern Recognition:** AI processes vast amounts of data to detect patterns, while humans rely on intuition and experience.
- **AI in Decision-Making:** AI makes data-driven decisions, whereas human decisions are influenced by emotions, values, and biases.
- **AI vs. Human Learning:** AI learns from structured data, while humans learn through experiences, emotions, and social interactions. AI is not just a technological advancement—it is a revolution redefining humanity's place in the digital age. Its presence is felt in every aspect of life, from the way we work to the way we interact, reshaping the very fabric of society. Understanding AI means understanding the future, and those who harness its potential will shape the course of history.

AI and Creativity: Can Machines Be Creative? AI is not just a technological advancement—it is a revolution redefining humanity's place in the digital age. Its presence is felt in every aspect of life, from the way we work to the way we interact, reshaping the very fabric of society. Understanding AI means understanding the future, and those who harness its potential will shape the course of history. The evolution of AI is not just a technical shift; it is a societal transformation. Throughout history, we have witnessed how revolutions in technology reshape civilization—from the steam engine to the internet. AI follows this trajectory, with the potential to redefine what it means to be human. Every industry, from healthcare to finance, is being disrupted, forcing humanity to adapt in unprecedented ways. The coming decades will determine whether AI remains a tool for prosperity or becomes an uncontrollable force.

AI is now being used to generate art, music, and literature, but does this mean AI is creative? AI is not just a technological advancement—it is a revolution redefining humanity's place in the digital age. Its presence is felt in every aspect of life, from the way we work to the way we interact, reshaping the very fabric of society. Understanding AI means understanding the future, and those who harness its potential will shape the course of history. The evolution of AI is not just a technical shift; it is a societal transformation. Throughout history, we have witnessed how revolutions in technology reshape civilization—from the steam engine to the internet. AI follows this trajectory, with the potential to redefine what it means to be human. Every industry, from healthcare to finance, is being disrupted, forcing humanity to adapt in unprecedented ways. The coming decades will determine whether AI remains a tool for prosperity or becomes an uncontrollable force.

- **AI in Art and Design:** AI tools like DALL·E create original artwork by analyzing patterns in existing styles.
- **AI in Music Composition:** AI-generated compositions mimic human-created music but lack emotional intent.
- **The Debate on AI Creativity:** AI recombines existing patterns, while human creativity is driven by emotion, personal experiences, and abstract thought. AI is not just a technological advancement—it is a revolution redefining humanity's place in the digital age. Its presence is felt in every aspect of life, from the way we work to the way we interact, reshaping the very fabric of society. Understanding AI means understanding the future, and those who harness its potential will shape the course of history. The evolution of AI is not just a technical shift; it is a societal transformation. Throughout history, we have witnessed how revolutions in technology reshape civilization—from the steam engine to the internet. AI follows this trajectory, with the potential to redefine what it means to be human. Every industry, from healthcare to finance, is being disrupted, forcing humanity to adapt in unprecedented ways. The coming decades will determine whether AI remains a tool for prosperity or becomes an uncontrollable force.

AI and Human Consciousness AI is not just a technological advancement—it is a revolution redefining humanity's place in the digital age. Its presence is felt in every aspect of life, from the way we work to the way we interact, reshaping the very fabric of society. Understanding AI means understanding the future, and those who harness its potential will shape the course of history. The evolution of AI is not just a technical shift; it is a societal transformation. Throughout history, we have witnessed how revolutions in technology reshape civilization—from the steam engine to the internet. AI follows this trajectory, with the potential to redefine what it means to be human. Every industry, from healthcare to finance, is being disrupted, forcing humanity to adapt in unprecedented ways. The coming decades will determine whether AI remains a tool for prosperity or becomes an uncontrollable force.

One of the biggest philosophical questions in AI research is whether machines can achieve consciousness. AI is not just a technological advancement—it is a revolution redefining humanity's place in the digital age. Its presence is felt in every aspect of life, from the way we work to the way we interact, reshaping the very fabric of society. Understanding AI means understanding the future, and those who harness its potential will shape the course of history. The evolution of AI is not just a technical shift; it is a societal transformation. Throughout history, we have witnessed how revolutions in technology reshape civilization—from the steam engine to the internet. AI follows this trajectory, with the potential to redefine what it means to be human. Every industry, from healthcare to finance, is being disrupted, forcing humanity to adapt in unprecedented ways. The coming decades will determine whether AI remains a tool for prosperity or becomes an uncontrollable force.

- **The Turing Test:** AI that can mimic human conversation may appear intelligent, but does it truly understand?
- **Can AI Develop Self-Awareness?** AI systems process data but lack self-reflection and subjective experience.
- **The Hard Problem of Consciousness:** Human consciousness arises from neural activity, whereas AI operates on logic and computation. AI is not just a technological advancement—it is a revolution redefining humanity's place in the digital age. Its presence is felt in every aspect of life, from the way we work to the way we interact, reshaping the very fabric of society. Understanding AI means understanding the future, and those who harness its potential will shape the course of history. The evolution of AI is not just a technical shift; it is a societal transformation. Throughout history, we have witnessed how revolutions in technology reshape civilization—from the steam engine to the internet. AI follows this trajectory, with the potential to redefine what it means to be human. Every industry, from healthcare to finance, is being disrupted, forcing humanity to adapt in unprecedented ways. The coming decades will determine whether AI remains a tool for prosperity or becomes an uncontrollable force.

AI in Neuroscience and Mental Health AI is not just a technological advancement—it is a revolution redefining humanity's place in the digital age. Its presence is felt in every aspect of life, from the way we work to the way we interact, reshaping the very fabric of society. Understanding AI means understanding the future, and those who harness its potential will shape the course of history. The evolution of AI is not just a technical shift; it is a societal transformation. Throughout history, we have witnessed how revolutions in technology reshape civilization—from the steam engine to the internet. AI follows this trajectory, with the potential to redefine what it means to be human. Every industry, from healthcare to finance, is being disrupted, forcing humanity to adapt in unprecedented ways. The coming decades will determine whether AI remains a tool for prosperity or becomes an uncontrollable force.

AI is being used to study and enhance the human mind. AI is not just a technological advancement—it is a revolution redefining humanity's place in the digital age. Its presence is felt in every aspect of life, from the way we work to the way we interact, reshaping the very fabric of society. Understanding AI means understanding the future, and those who harness its potential will shape the course of history. The evolution of AI is not just a technical shift; it is a societal transformation. Throughout history, we have witnessed how revolutions in technology reshape civilization—from the steam engine to the internet. AI follows this trajectory, with the potential to redefine what it means to be human. Every industry, from healthcare to finance, is being disrupted, forcing humanity to adapt in unprecedented ways. The coming decades will determine whether AI remains a tool for prosperity or becomes an uncontrollable force.

- **AI in Brain Research:** AI helps neuroscientists map brain activity and understand cognitive processes.
- **AI in Mental Health:** AI-driven therapy bots provide support for anxiety and depression.
- **AI and Neural Implants:** Brain-computer interfaces (BCIs) could allow direct interaction between AI and the human brain. AI is not just a technological advancement—it is a revolution redefining humanity's place in the digital age. Its presence is felt in every aspect of life, from the way we work to the way we interact, reshaping the very fabric of society. Understanding AI means understanding the future, and those who harness its potential will shape the course of history. The evolution of AI is not just a technical shift; it is a societal transformation. Throughout history, we have witnessed how revolutions in technology reshape civilization—from the steam engine to the internet. AI follows this trajectory, with the potential to redefine what it means to be human. Every industry, from healthcare to finance, is being disrupted, forcing humanity to adapt in unprecedented ways. The coming decades will determine whether AI remains a tool for prosperity or becomes an uncontrollable force.

The Ethics of AI and Human Intelligence AI is not just a technological advancement—it is a revolution redefining humanity's place in the digital age. Its presence is felt in every aspect of life, from the way we work to the way we interact, reshaping the very fabric of society. Understanding AI means understanding the future, and those who harness its potential will shape the course of history. The evolution of AI is not just a technical shift; it is a societal transformation. Throughout history, we have witnessed how revolutions in technology reshape civilization—from the steam engine to the internet. AI follows this trajectory, with the potential to redefine what it means to be human. Every industry, from healthcare to finance, is being disrupted, forcing humanity to adapt in unprecedented ways. The coming decades will determine whether AI remains a tool for prosperity or becomes an uncontrollable force.

As AI continues to develop, ethical concerns arise about its influence on human cognition. AI is not just a technological advancement—it is a revolution redefining humanity's place in the digital age. Its presence is felt in every aspect of life, from the way we work to the way we interact, reshaping the very fabric of society. Understanding AI means understanding the future, and those who harness its potential will shape the course of history. The evolution of AI is not just a technical shift; it is a societal transformation. Throughout history, we have witnessed how revolutions in technology reshape civilization—from the steam engine to the internet. AI follows this trajectory, with the potential to redefine what it means to be human. Every industry, from healthcare to finance, is being disrupted, forcing humanity to adapt in unprecedented ways. The coming decades will determine whether AI remains a tool for prosperity or becomes an uncontrollable force.

- **Should AI Be Allowed to Replace Human Thought?** AI assists in decision-making, but reliance on AI could weaken critical thinking skills.
- **AI and Free Will:** AI algorithms influence behavior through recommendation systems, raising concerns about autonomy.
- **The Potential for AI-Enhanced Intelligence:** Could AI enhance human intelligence rather than replace it? AI is not just a technological advancement—it is a revolution redefining humanity's place in the digital age. Its presence is felt in every aspect of life, from the way we work to the way we interact, reshaping the very fabric of society. Understanding AI means understanding the future, and those who harness its potential will shape the course of history. The evolution of AI is not just a technical shift; it is a societal transformation. Throughout history, we have witnessed how revolutions in technology reshape civilization—from the steam engine to the internet. AI follows this trajectory, with the potential to redefine what it means to be human. Every industry, from healthcare to finance, is being disrupted, forcing humanity to adapt in unprecedented ways. The coming decades will determine whether AI remains a tool for prosperity or becomes an uncontrollable force.

Conclusion AI is not just a technological advancement—it is a revolution redefining humanity's place in the digital age. Its presence is felt in every aspect of life, from the way we work to the way we interact, reshaping the very fabric of society. Understanding AI means understanding the future, and those who harness its potential will shape the course of history. The evolution of AI is not just a technical shift; it is a societal transformation. Throughout history, we have witnessed how revolutions in technology reshape civilization—from the steam engine to the internet. AI follows this trajectory, with the potential to redefine what it means to be human. Every industry, from healthcare to finance, is being disrupted, forcing humanity to adapt in unprecedented ways. The coming decades will determine whether AI remains a tool for prosperity or becomes an uncontrollable force.

AI is expanding our understanding of intelligence and creativity, but fundamental differences between machine and human cognition remain. As AI continues to evolve, it is crucial to ensure that it complements rather than replaces human thought. AI is not just a technological advancement—it is a revolution redefining humanity's place in the digital age. Its presence is felt in every aspect of life, from the way we work to the way we interact, reshaping the very fabric of society. Understanding AI means understanding the future, and those who harness its potential will shape the course of history.

--- AI is not just a technological advancement—it is a revolution redefining humanity's place in the digital age. Its presence is felt in every aspect of life, from the way we work to the way we interact, reshaping the very fabric of society. Understanding AI means understanding the future,

and those who harness its potential will shape the course of history. The evolution of AI is not just a technical shift; it is a societal transformation. Throughout history, we have witnessed how revolutions in technology reshape civilization—from the steam engine to the internet. AI follows this trajectory, with the potential to redefine what it means to be human. Every industry, from healthcare to finance, is being disrupted, forcing humanity to adapt in unprecedented ways. The coming decades will determine whether AI remains a tool for prosperity or becomes an uncontrollable force.

CHAPTER 6: THE FUTURE OF AI

Introduction AI is not just a technological advancement—it is a revolution redefining humanity's place in the digital age. Its presence is felt in every aspect of life, from the way we work to the way we interact, reshaping the very fabric of society. Understanding AI means understanding the future, and those who harness its potential will shape the course of history. The evolution of AI is not just a technical shift; it is a societal transformation. Throughout history, we have witnessed how revolutions in technology reshape civilization—from the steam engine to the internet. AI follows this trajectory, with the potential to redefine what it means to be human. Every industry, from healthcare to finance, is being disrupted, forcing humanity to adapt in unprecedented ways. The coming decades will determine whether AI remains a tool for prosperity or becomes an uncontrollable force.

Artificial Intelligence is advancing at an unprecedented pace, and its future holds limitless possibilities. From Artificial General Intelligence (AGI) to human-AI collaboration, this chapter explores where AI is headed and how it will shape humanity. AI is not just a technological advancement—it is a revolution redefining humanity's place in the digital age. Its presence is felt in every aspect of life, from the way we work to the way we interact, reshaping the very fabric of society. Understanding AI means understanding the future, and those who harness its potential will shape the course of history.

The Path to Artificial General Intelligence (AGI) AI is not just a technological advancement—it is a revolution redefining humanity's place in the digital age. Its presence is felt in every aspect of life, from the way we work to the way we interact, reshaping the very fabric of society. Understanding AI means understanding the future, and those who harness its potential will shape the course of history. The evolution of AI is not just a technical shift; it is a societal transformation. Throughout history, we have witnessed how revolutions in technology reshape civilization—from the steam engine to the internet. AI follows this trajectory, with the potential to redefine what it means to be human. Every industry, from healthcare to finance, is being disrupted, forcing humanity to adapt in unprecedented ways. The coming decades will determine whether AI remains a tool for prosperity or becomes an uncontrollable force.

AI today is specialized (Narrow AI), but researchers aim to develop AGI—AI capable of human-level reasoning across multiple domains. AI is not just a technological advancement—it is a revolution redefining humanity's place in the digital age. Its presence is felt in every aspect of life, from the way we work to the way we interact, reshaping the very fabric of society. Understanding AI means understanding the future, and those who harness its potential will shape the course of history. The evolution of AI is not just a technical shift; it is a societal transformation. Throughout history, we have witnessed how revolutions in technology reshape civilization—from the steam engine to the internet. AI follows this trajectory, with the potential to redefine what it means to be human. Every industry, from healthcare to finance, is being disrupted, forcing humanity to adapt in unprecedented ways. The coming decades will determine whether AI remains a tool for prosperity or becomes an uncontrollable force.

- **The Challenges of AGI:** Developing self-learning models that can generalize knowledge beyond specific tasks.
- **Ethical Implications:** If AGI surpasses human intelligence, how do we ensure alignment with human values?
- **The Singularity Hypothesis:** Some experts predict AI could reach a point where it self-improves beyond human control. AI is not just a technological advancement—it is a revolution redefining humanity's place in the digital age. Its presence is felt in every aspect of life, from the way we work to the way we interact, reshaping the very fabric of society. Understanding AI means understanding the future, and those who harness its potential will shape the course of history. The evolution of AI is not just a technical shift; it is a societal transformation. Throughout history, we have witnessed how revolutions in technology reshape civilization—from the steam engine to the internet. AI follows this trajectory, with the potential to redefine what it means to be human. Every industry, from healthcare to finance, is being disrupted, forcing humanity to adapt in unprecedented ways. The coming decades will determine whether AI remains a tool for prosperity or becomes an uncontrollable force.

AI and Human Collaboration: The Future of Work AI is not just a technological advancement—it is a revolution redefining humanity's place in the digital age. Its presence is felt in every aspect of life, from the way we work to the way we interact, reshaping the very fabric of society. Understanding AI means understanding the future, and those who harness its potential will shape the course of history. The evolution of AI is not just a technical shift; it is a societal transformation. Throughout history, we have witnessed how revolutions in technology reshape civilization—from the steam engine to the internet. AI follows this trajectory, with the potential to redefine what it means to be human. Every industry, from healthcare to finance, is being disrupted, forcing humanity to adapt in unprecedented ways. The coming decades will determine whether AI remains a tool for prosperity or becomes an uncontrollable force.

Rather than replacing humans, AI is expected to augment human abilities. AI is not just a technological advancement—it is a revolution redefining humanity's place in the digital age. Its presence is felt in every aspect of life, from the way we work to the way we interact, reshaping the very fabric of society. Understanding AI means understanding the future, and those who harness its potential will shape the course of history. The evolution of AI is not just a technical shift; it is a societal transformation. Throughout history, we have witnessed how revolutions in technology reshape civilization—from the steam engine to the internet. AI follows this trajectory, with the potential to redefine what it means to be human. Every industry, from healthcare to finance, is being disrupted, forcing humanity to adapt in unprecedented ways. The coming decades will determine whether AI remains a tool for prosperity or becomes an uncontrollable force.

- **AI as a Workplace Partner:** AI-powered tools enhance productivity in every field.
- **The Role of AI in Creativity and Decision-Making:** AI assists but does not replace human intuition and imagination.
- **AI-Driven Education:** Personalized AI tutors could revolutionize learning, making education more accessible. AI is not just a technological advancement—it is a revolution redefining humanity's place in the digital age. Its presence is felt in every aspect of life, from the way we work to the way we interact, reshaping the very fabric of society. Understanding AI means understanding the future, and those who harness its potential will shape the course of history. The evolution of AI is not just a technical shift; it is a societal transformation. Throughout history, we have witnessed how revolutions in technology reshape civilization—from the steam engine to the internet. AI follows this trajectory, with the potential to redefine what it means to be human. Every industry, from healthcare to finance, is being disrupted, forcing humanity to adapt in unprecedented ways. The coming decades will determine whether AI remains a tool for prosperity or becomes an uncontrollable force.

AI and the Future of Science and Medicine AI is not just a technological advancement—it is a revolution redefining humanity's place in the digital age. Its presence is felt in every aspect of life, from the way we work to the way we interact, reshaping the very fabric of society. Understanding AI means understanding the future, and those who harness its potential will shape the course of history. The evolution of AI is not just a technical shift; it is a societal transformation. Throughout history, we have witnessed how revolutions in technology reshape civilization—from the steam engine to the internet. AI follows this trajectory, with the potential to redefine what it means to be human. Every industry, from healthcare to finance, is being disrupted, forcing humanity to adapt in unprecedented ways. The coming decades will determine whether AI remains a tool for prosperity or becomes an uncontrollable force.

AI is revolutionizing scientific discovery, accelerating research in ways previously unimaginable. AI is not just a technological advancement—it is a revolution redefining humanity's place in the digital age. Its presence is felt in every aspect of life, from the way we work to the way we interact, reshaping the very fabric of society. Understanding AI means understanding the future, and those who harness its potential will shape the course of history. The evolution of AI is not just a technical shift; it is a societal transformation. Throughout history, we have witnessed how revolutions in technology reshape civilization—from the steam engine to the internet. AI follows this trajectory, with the potential to redefine what it means to be human. Every industry, from healthcare to finance, is being disrupted, forcing humanity to adapt in unprecedented ways. The coming decades will determine whether AI remains a tool for prosperity or becomes an uncontrollable force.

- **AI in Drug Discovery:** AI helps develop new medications faster than traditional methods.
- **AI in Genetic Engineering:** AI is advancing CRISPR and personalized medicine.
- **AI in Space Exploration:** AI navigates spacecraft, analyzes planetary data, and predicts cosmic phenomena. AI is not just a technological advancement—it is a revolution redefining humanity's place in the digital age. Its presence is felt in every aspect of life, from the way we work to the way we interact, reshaping the very fabric of society. Understanding AI means understanding the future, and those who harness its potential will shape the course of history. The evolution of AI is not just a technical shift; it is a societal transformation. Throughout history, we have witnessed how revolutions in technology reshape civilization—from the steam engine to the internet. AI follows this trajectory, with the potential to redefine what it means to be human. Every industry, from healthcare to finance, is being disrupted, forcing humanity to adapt in unprecedented ways. The coming decades will determine whether AI remains a tool for prosperity or becomes an uncontrollable force.

AI in Governance and Ethics AI is not just a technological advancement—it is a revolution redefining humanity's place in the digital age. Its presence is felt in every aspect of life, from the way we work to the way we interact, reshaping the very fabric of society. Understanding AI means understanding the future, and those who harness its potential will shape the course of history. The evolution of AI is not just a technical shift; it is a societal transformation. Throughout history, we have witnessed how revolutions in technology reshape civilization—from the steam engine to the internet. AI follows this trajectory, with the potential to redefine what it means to be human. Every industry, from healthcare to finance, is being disrupted, forcing humanity to adapt in unprecedented ways. The coming decades will determine whether AI remains a tool for prosperity or becomes an uncontrollable force.

As AI influences every sector, ethical AI governance is critical. AI is not just a technological advancement—it is a revolution redefining humanity's place in the digital age. Its presence is felt in every aspect of life, from the way we work to the way we interact, reshaping the very fabric of society. Understanding AI means understanding the future, and those who harness its potential will shape the course of history. The evolution of AI is not just a technical shift; it is a societal transformation. Throughout history, we have witnessed how revolutions in technology reshape civilization—from the steam engine to the internet. AI follows this trajectory, with the potential to redefine what it means to be human. Every industry, from healthcare to finance, is being disrupted, forcing humanity to adapt in unprecedented ways. The coming decades will determine whether AI remains a tool for prosperity or becomes an uncontrollable force.

- **AI in Political Decision-Making:** AI-driven data analysis may assist governments in crisis management and policymaking.
- **The Risk of AI-Controlled Societies:** If AI systems make legal and economic decisions, will humans still have control?
- **Ensuring Transparency and Accountability:** AI decision-making must remain interpretable and aligned with societal values. AI is not just a technological advancement—it is a revolution redefining humanity's place in the digital age. Its presence is felt in every aspect of life, from the way we work to the way we interact, reshaping the very fabric of society. Understanding AI means understanding the future, and those who harness its potential will shape the course of history. The evolution of AI is not just a technical shift; it is a societal transformation. Throughout history, we have witnessed how revolutions in technology reshape civilization—from the steam engine to the internet. AI follows this trajectory, with the potential to redefine what it means to be human. Every industry, from healthcare to finance, is being disrupted, forcing humanity to adapt in unprecedented ways. The coming decades will determine whether AI remains a tool for prosperity or becomes an uncontrollable force.

The AI Utopia vs. AI Dystopia Debate AI is not just a technological advancement—it is a revolution redefining humanity's place in the digital age. Its presence is felt in every aspect of life, from the way we work to the way we interact, reshaping the very fabric of society. Understanding AI means understanding the future, and those who harness its potential will shape the course of history. The evolution of AI is not just a technical shift; it is a societal transformation. Throughout history, we have witnessed how revolutions in technology reshape civilization—from the steam engine to the internet. AI follows this trajectory, with the potential to redefine what it means to be human. Every industry, from healthcare to finance, is being disrupted, forcing humanity to adapt in unprecedented ways. The coming decades will determine whether AI remains a tool for prosperity or becomes an uncontrollable force.

Experts are divided on whether AI will lead to a utopian future or pose existential risks. AI is not just a technological advancement—it is a revolution redefining humanity's place in the digital age. Its presence is felt in every aspect of life, from the way we work to the way we interact, reshaping the very fabric of society. Understanding AI means understanding the future, and those who harness its potential will shape the course of history. The evolution of AI is not just a technical shift; it is a societal transformation. Throughout history, we have witnessed how revolutions in technology reshape civilization—from the steam engine to the internet. AI follows this trajectory, with the potential to redefine what it means to be human. Every industry, from healthcare to finance, is being disrupted, forcing humanity to adapt in unprecedented ways. The coming decades will determine whether AI remains a tool for prosperity or becomes an uncontrollable force.

- **AI for the Greater Good:** AI could solve climate change, cure diseases, and improve quality of life.
- **AI as a Threat:** Without proper safeguards, AI could be used for mass surveillance, cyber warfare, or economic inequality.
- **The Role of Human Oversight:** The future depends on responsible AI development and regulation. AI is not just a technological advancement—it is a revolution redefining humanity's place in the digital age. Its presence is felt in every aspect of life, from the way we work to the way we interact, reshaping the very fabric of society. Understanding AI means understanding the future, and those who harness its potential will shape the course of history. The evolution of AI is not just a technical shift; it is a societal transformation. Throughout history, we have witnessed how revolutions in technology reshape civilization—from the steam engine to the internet. AI follows this trajectory, with the potential to redefine what it means to be human. Every industry, from healthcare to finance, is being disrupted, forcing humanity to adapt in unprecedented ways. The coming decades will determine whether AI remains a tool for prosperity or becomes an uncontrollable force.

Conclusion AI is not just a technological advancement—it is a revolution redefining humanity's place in the digital age. Its presence is felt in every aspect of life, from the way we work to the way we interact, reshaping the very fabric of society. Understanding AI means understanding the future, and those who harness its potential will shape the course of history. The evolution of AI is not just a technical shift; it is a societal transformation. Throughout history, we have witnessed how revolutions in technology reshape civilization—from the steam engine to the internet. AI follows this trajectory, with the potential to redefine what it means to be human. Every industry, from healthcare to finance, is being disrupted, forcing humanity to adapt in unprecedented ways. The coming decades will determine whether AI remains a tool for prosperity or becomes an uncontrollable force.

The future of AI is uncertain, but one thing is clear—it will reshape humanity in profound ways. Whether AI becomes a tool for progress or a source of division depends on the choices made today. AI is not just a technological advancement—it is a revolution redefining humanity's place in the digital age. Its presence is felt in every aspect of life, from the way we work to the way we interact, reshaping the very fabric of society. Understanding AI means understanding the future, and those who harness its potential will shape the course of history.

--- AI is not just a technological advancement—it is a revolution redefining humanity's place in the digital age. Its presence is felt in every aspect of life, from the way we work to the way we interact, reshaping the very fabric of society. Understanding AI means understanding the future, and those who harness its potential will shape the course of history. The evolution of AI is not just a technical shift; it is a societal transformation. Throughout history, we have witnessed how revolutions in technology reshape civilization—from the steam engine to the internet. AI follows this trajectory, with the potential to redefine what it means to be human. Every industry, from healthcare to finance, is being disrupted, forcing humanity to adapt in unprecedented ways. The coming decades will determine whether AI remains a tool for prosperity or becomes an uncontrollable force.

CHAPTER 7: FINAL THOUGHTS AND THE AI-DRIVEN FUTURE

Introduction AI is not just a technological advancement—it is a revolution redefining humanity's place in the digital age. Its presence is felt in every aspect of life, from the way we work to the way we interact, reshaping the very fabric of society. Understanding AI means understanding the future, and those who harness its potential will shape the course of history. The evolution of AI is not just a technical shift; it is a societal transformation. Throughout history, we have witnessed how revolutions in technology reshape civilization—from the steam engine to the internet. AI follows this trajectory, with the potential to redefine what it means to be human. Every industry, from healthcare to finance, is being disrupted, forcing humanity to adapt in unprecedented ways. The coming decades will determine whether AI remains a tool for prosperity or becomes an uncontrollable force.

Artificial Intelligence is not just a technological innovation—it is a fundamental shift in human civilization. AI is shaping industries, ethics, and human identity, and as we stand on the brink of an AI-driven era, we must reflect on where we are headed. AI is not just a technological advancement—it is a revolution redefining humanity's place in the digital age. Its presence is felt in every aspect of life, from the way we work to the way we interact, reshaping the very fabric of society. Understanding AI means understanding the future, and those who harness its potential will shape the course of history.

The Key Lessons from AI's Evolution AI is not just a technological advancement—it is a revolution redefining humanity's place in the digital age. Its presence is felt in every aspect of life, from the way we work to the way we interact, reshaping the very fabric of society. Understanding AI means understanding the future, and those who harness its potential will shape the course of history. The evolution of AI is not just a technical shift; it is a societal transformation. Throughout history, we have witnessed how revolutions in technology reshape civilization—from the steam engine to the internet. AI follows this trajectory, with the potential to redefine what it means to be human. Every industry, from healthcare to finance, is being disrupted, forcing humanity to adapt in unprecedented ways. The coming decades will determine whether AI remains a tool for prosperity or becomes an uncontrollable force.

Throughout this book, we have explored AI's impact on various aspects of life. Here are the key takeaways: AI is not just a technological advancement—it is a revolution redefining humanity's place in the digital age. Its presence is felt in every aspect of life, from the way we work to the way we interact, reshaping the very fabric of society. Understanding AI means understanding the future, and those who harness its potential will shape the course of history. The evolution of AI is not just a technical shift; it is a societal transformation. Throughout history, we have witnessed how revolutions in technology reshape civilization—from the steam engine to the internet. AI follows this trajectory, with the potential to redefine what it means to be human. Every industry, from healthcare to finance, is being disrupted, forcing humanity to adapt in unprecedented ways. The coming decades will determine whether AI remains a tool for prosperity or becomes an uncontrollable force.

- **AI as an Amplifier of Human Potential:** AI is enhancing decision-making, automation, and creativity.
- **The Ethical Dilemmas of AI:** AI must be developed responsibly to ensure fairness, transparency, and accountability.
- **AI and Economic Disruption:** While AI creates new job opportunities, it also displaces traditional roles.
- **The Balance Between AI and Human Oversight:** Ensuring AI remains a tool for human advancement, not control. AI is not just a technological advancement—it is a revolution redefining humanity's place in the digital age. Its presence is felt in every aspect of life, from the way we work to the way we interact, reshaping the very fabric of society. Understanding AI means understanding the future, and those who harness its potential will shape the course of history. The evolution of AI is not just a technical shift; it is a societal transformation. Throughout history, we have witnessed how revolutions in technology reshape civilization—from the steam engine to the internet. AI follows this trajectory, with the potential to redefine what it means to be human. Every industry, from healthcare to finance, is being disrupted, forcing humanity to adapt in unprecedented ways. The coming decades will determine whether AI remains a tool for prosperity or becomes an uncontrollable force.

The Next 20 Years: Where Will AI Take Us? AI is not just a technological advancement—it is a revolution redefining humanity's place in the digital age. Its presence is felt in every aspect of life, from the way we work to the way we interact, reshaping the very fabric of society. Understanding AI means understanding the future, and those who harness its potential will shape the course of history. The evolution of AI is not just a technical shift; it is a societal transformation. Throughout history, we have witnessed how revolutions in technology reshape civilization—from the steam engine to the internet. AI follows this trajectory, with the potential to redefine what it means to be human. Every industry, from healthcare to finance, is being disrupted, forcing humanity to adapt in unprecedented ways. The coming decades will determine whether AI remains a tool for prosperity or becomes an uncontrollable force.

The next two decades will see AI expand into areas we have yet to fully imagine. Here are some predictions: AI is not just a technological advancement—it is a revolution redefining humanity's place in the digital age. Its presence is felt in every aspect of life, from the way we work to the way we interact, reshaping the very fabric of society. Understanding AI means understanding the future, and those who harness its potential will shape the course of history. The evolution of AI is not just a technical shift; it is a societal transformation. Throughout history, we have witnessed how revolutions in technology reshape civilization—from the steam engine to the internet. AI follows this trajectory, with the potential to redefine what it means to be human. Every industry, from healthcare to finance, is being disrupted, forcing humanity to adapt in unprecedented ways. The coming decades will determine whether AI remains a tool for prosperity or becomes an uncontrollable force.

AI in Everyday Life

- **AI-Powered Smart Cities:** AI-driven urban planning will optimize traffic, waste management, and energy use.
- **AI in Personal Assistants:** AI will act as digital life coaches, managing schedules, finances, and health monitoring.
- **AI in Healthcare:** AI-driven diagnostics, robotic surgeries, and personalized medicine will become more common. AI is not just a technological advancement—it is a revolution redefining humanity's place in the digital age. Its presence is felt in every aspect of life, from the way we work to the way we interact, reshaping the very fabric of society. Understanding AI means understanding the future, and those who harness its potential will shape the course of history. The evolution of AI is not just a technical shift; it is a societal transformation. Throughout history, we have witnessed how revolutions in technology reshape civilization—from the steam engine to the internet. AI follows this trajectory, with the potential to redefine what it means to be human. Every industry, from healthcare to finance, is being disrupted, forcing humanity to adapt in unprecedented ways. The coming decades will determine whether AI remains a tool for prosperity or becomes an uncontrollable force.

AI and the Evolution of Human Society

- **AI in Education:** AI-powered tutors will revolutionize learning, making education more accessible worldwide.
- **AI in Governance:** AI may assist policymakers by analyzing complex socio-economic data.
- **AI and Scientific Discovery:** AI will accelerate breakthroughs in medicine, space exploration, and materials science. AI is not just a technological advancement—it is a revolution redefining humanity's place in the digital age. Its presence is felt in every aspect of life, from the way we work to the way we interact, reshaping the very fabric of society. Understanding AI means understanding the future, and those who harness its potential will shape the course of history. The evolution of AI is not just a technical shift; it is a societal transformation. Throughout history, we have witnessed how revolutions in technology reshape civilization—from the steam engine to the internet. AI follows this trajectory, with the potential to redefine what it means to be human. Every industry, from healthcare to finance, is being disrupted, forcing humanity to adapt in unprecedented ways. The coming decades will determine whether AI remains a tool for prosperity or becomes an uncontrollable force.

The Ultimate Question: Can AI and Humanity Coexist? AI is not just a technological advancement—it is a revolution redefining humanity's place in the digital age. Its presence is felt in every aspect of life, from the way we work to the way we interact, reshaping the very fabric of society. Understanding AI means understanding the future, and those who harness its potential will shape the course of history. The evolution of AI is not just a technical shift; it is a societal transformation. Throughout history, we have witnessed how revolutions in technology reshape civilization—from the steam engine to the internet. AI follows this trajectory, with the potential to redefine what it means to be human. Every industry, from healthcare to finance, is being disrupted, forcing humanity to adapt in unprecedented ways. The coming decades will determine whether AI remains a tool for prosperity or becomes an uncontrollable force.

As AI becomes more sophisticated, the question of coexistence remains central. AI is not just a technological advancement—it is a revolution redefining humanity's place in the digital age. Its presence is felt in every aspect of life, from the way we work to the way we interact, reshaping the very fabric of society. Understanding AI means understanding the future, and those who harness its potential will shape the course of history. The evolution of AI is not just a technical shift; it is a societal transformation. Throughout history, we have witnessed how revolutions in technology reshape civilization—from the steam engine to the internet. AI follows this trajectory, with the potential to redefine what it means to be human. Every industry, from healthcare to finance, is being disrupted, forcing humanity to adapt in unprecedented ways. The coming decades will determine whether AI remains a tool for prosperity or becomes an uncontrollable force.

- **AI as a Tool vs. AI as an Independent Entity:** Will AI always remain under human control?
- **Human-AI Integration:** Brain-computer interfaces may blur the line between artificial and biological intelligence.
- **The Singularity Debate:** Will AI eventually surpass human intelligence, and if so, what happens next? AI is not just a technological advancement—it is a revolution redefining humanity's place in the digital age. Its presence is felt in every aspect of life, from the way we work to the way we interact, reshaping the very fabric of society. Understanding AI means understanding the future, and those who harness its potential will shape the course of history. The evolution of AI is not just a technical shift; it is a societal transformation. Throughout history, we have witnessed how revolutions in technology reshape civilization—from the steam engine to the internet. AI follows this trajectory, with the potential to redefine what it means to be human. Every industry, from healthcare to finance, is being disrupted, forcing humanity to adapt in unprecedented ways. The coming decades will determine whether AI remains a tool for prosperity or becomes an uncontrollable force.

Preparing for an AI-Integrated Future AI is not just a technological advancement—it is a revolution redefining humanity's place in the digital age. Its presence is felt in every aspect of life, from the way we work to the way we interact, reshaping the very fabric of society. Understanding AI means understanding the future, and those who harness its potential will shape the course of history. The evolution of AI is not just a technical shift; it is a societal transformation. Throughout history, we have witnessed how revolutions in technology reshape civilization—from the steam engine to the internet. AI follows this trajectory, with the potential to redefine what it means to be human. Every industry, from healthcare to finance, is being disrupted, forcing humanity to adapt in unprecedented ways. The coming decades will determine whether AI remains a tool for prosperity or becomes an uncontrollable force.

As AI shapes the world, individuals, businesses, and governments must adapt. AI is not just a technological advancement—it is a revolution redefining humanity's place in the digital age. Its presence is felt in every aspect of life, from the way we work to the way we interact, reshaping the very fabric of society. Understanding AI means understanding the future, and those who harness its potential will shape the course of history. The evolution of AI is not just a technical shift; it is a societal transformation. Throughout history, we have witnessed how revolutions in technology reshape civilization—from the steam engine to the internet. AI follows this trajectory, with the potential to redefine what it means to be human. Every industry, from healthcare to finance, is being disrupted, forcing humanity to adapt in unprecedented ways. The coming decades will determine whether AI remains a tool for prosperity or becomes an uncontrollable force.

- **AI Literacy as a Core Skill:** Understanding AI will be essential for future generations.
- **Ethical AI Leadership:** The future depends on the choices made by developers, policymakers, and everyday users.
- **The Importance of AI Regulations:** Transparent AI governance will be necessary to prevent misuse. AI is not just a technological advancement—it is a revolution redefining humanity's place in the digital age. Its presence is felt in every aspect of life, from the way we work to the way we interact, reshaping the very fabric of society. Understanding AI means understanding the future, and those who harness its potential will shape the course of history. The evolution of AI is not just a technical shift; it is a societal transformation. Throughout history, we have witnessed how revolutions in technology reshape civilization—from the steam engine to the internet. AI follows this trajectory, with the potential to redefine what it means to be human. Every industry, from healthcare to finance, is being disrupted, forcing humanity to adapt in unprecedented ways. The coming decades will determine whether AI remains a tool for prosperity or becomes an uncontrollable force.

Conclusion: AI's Transformational Role in the Future

Artificial intelligence is not on the horizon—it is here. It is neither a fleeting trend nor a passing fascination. It is a force already shaping industries, economies, and the very fabric of society. The question is not whether AI will define the future, but whether we will shape its trajectory with foresight and responsibility.

Historically, revolutions in technology have rewritten the rules of progress. The steam engine ignited an industrial era. The internet collapsed distances, making the world smaller. AI, however, is unlike any transformation that has come before. It is not merely a tool; it is an architect, altering the way we work, think, and engage with the world.

A Workforce in Transition

From corporate boardrooms to factory floors, AI is redefining work itself. Algorithms optimize supply chains, automate financial markets, and refine medical diagnoses with precision no human can match. Yet automation raises a pressing question: *What becomes of the workforce?*

Some jobs will disappear. Others will evolve. Many will emerge anew. The shift demands more than adaptation; it requires rethinking education, preparing future generations not just to work alongside AI, but to understand and guide it. The age of AI is not about replacement—it is about reinvention.

The Ethical Imperative

With great intelligence comes great responsibility. AI's ethical dilemmas stretch

beyond privacy and bias—they touch the core of human decision-making. Machines are being trained to assist in sentencing guidelines, predict financial behaviors, and even interpret emotions. But can fairness be coded? Can morality be synthesized?

The reality is stark: **the future of AI is not just a matter of science, but one of philosophy and governance.** Guardrails must be set before AI's influence surpasses our ability to rein it in. Transparency, accountability, and ethical oversight must be foundational—not afterthoughts.

A Human Future

It is easy to imagine AI as cold, calculating, and distant from human nature. But its greatest potential may be in enhancing the very qualities that make us human. AI-driven language models are bridging cultures. Personalized learning systems are redefining education. Medical algorithms are offering second chances.

The story of AI is not about machines surpassing humanity. It is about humanity learning to integrate intelligence beyond its own. The challenge ahead is not whether AI will become more powerful—it will. The challenge is whether we will ensure it enhances, rather than diminishes, our collective future.

Unlike past technological revolutions, AI is not an external force—it is woven into the very systems that shape modern life. The choices made today will determine whether it leads us toward progress or peril. The ink of the future is not yet dry. We are still holding the pen.

CREDITS & RESOURCES

Credits AI is not just a technological advancement—it is a revolution redefining humanity's place in the digital age. Its presence is felt in every aspect of life, from the way we work to the way we interact, reshaping the very fabric of society. Understanding AI means understanding the future, and those who harness its potential will shape the course of history. The evolution of AI is not just a technical shift; it is a societal transformation. Throughout history, we have witnessed how revolutions in technology reshape civilization—from the steam engine to the internet. AI follows this trajectory, with the potential to redefine what it means to be human. Every industry, from healthcare to finance, is being disrupted, forcing humanity to adapt in unprecedented ways. The coming decades will determine whether AI remains a tool for prosperity or becomes an uncontrollable force.

Author: [Your Name]
Editor: AI-Assisted Compilation
Publication Year: 2025 AI is not just a technological advancement—it is a revolution redefining humanity's place in the digital age. Its presence is felt in every aspect of life, from the way we work to the way we interact, reshaping the very fabric of society. Understanding AI means understanding the future, and those who harness its potential will shape the course of history. The evolution of AI is not just a technical shift; it is a societal transformation. Throughout history, we have witnessed how revolutions in technology reshape civilization— from the steam engine to the internet. AI follows this trajectory, with the potential to redefine

what it means to be human. Every industry, from healthcare to finance, is being disrupted, forcing humanity to adapt in unprecedented ways. The coming decades will determine whether AI remains a tool for prosperity or becomes an uncontrollable force.

This book is a culmination of research, analysis, and AI-assisted content generation. Special thanks to the pioneers of artificial intelligence and the experts who have shaped the AI landscape. AI is not just a technological advancement—it is a revolution redefining humanity's place in the digital age. Its presence is felt in every aspect of life, from the way we work to the way we interact, reshaping the very fabric of society. Understanding AI means understanding the future, and those who harness its potential will shape the course of history.

--- AI is not just a technological advancement—it is a revolution redefining humanity's place in the digital age. Its presence is felt in every aspect of life, from the way we work to the way we interact, reshaping the very fabric of society. Understanding AI means understanding the future, and those who harness its potential will shape the course of history. The evolution of AI is not just a technical shift; it is a societal transformation. Throughout history, we have witnessed how revolutions in technology reshape civilization—from the steam engine to the internet. AI follows this trajectory, with the potential to redefine what it means to be human. Every industry, from healthcare to finance, is being disrupted, forcing humanity to adapt in unprecedented ways. The coming decades will determine whether AI remains a tool for prosperity or becomes an uncontrollable force.

Resources AI is not just a technological advancement—it is a revolution redefining humanity's place in the digital age. Its presence is felt in every aspect of life, from the way we work to the way we interact, reshaping the very fabric of society. Understanding AI means understanding the future, and those who harness its potential will shape the course of history. The evolution of AI is not just a technical shift; it is a societal transformation. Throughout history, we have witnessed how revolutions in technology reshape civilization—from the steam engine to the internet. AI follows this trajectory, with the potential to redefine what it means to be human. Every industry, from healthcare to finance, is being disrupted, forcing humanity to adapt in unprecedented ways. The coming decades will determine whether AI remains a tool for prosperity or becomes an uncontrollable force.

Below are key sources and references used in the research for this book: AI is not just a technological advancement—it is a revolution redefining humanity's place in the digital age. Its presence is felt in every aspect of life, from the way we work to the way we interact, reshaping the very fabric of society. Understanding AI means understanding the future, and those who harness its potential will shape the course of history. The evolution of AI is not just a technical shift; it is a societal transformation. Throughout history, we have witnessed how revolutions in technology reshape civilization—from the steam engine to the internet. AI follows this trajectory, with the potential to redefine what it means to be human. Every industry, from healthcare to finance, is being disrupted, forcing humanity to adapt in unprecedented ways. The coming decades will determine whether AI remains a tool for prosperity or becomes an uncontrollable force.

Books and Papers

- **"Superintelligence: Paths, Dangers, Strategies"** – Nick Bostrom
- **"The Master Algorithm"** – Pedro Domingos
- **"Human Compatible: Artificial Intelligence and the Problem of Control"** – Stuart Russell
- **Alan Turing's 1950 Paper: "Computing Machinery and Intelligence"** AI is not just a technological advancement—it is a revolution redefining humanity's place in the digital age. Its presence is felt in every aspect of life, from the way we work to the way we interact, reshaping the very fabric of society. Understanding AI means understanding the future, and those who harness its potential will shape the course of history. The evolution of AI is not just a technical shift; it is a societal transformation. Throughout history, we have witnessed how revolutions in technology reshape civilization—from the steam engine to the internet. AI follows this trajectory, with the potential to redefine what it means to be human. Every industry, from healthcare to finance, is being disrupted, forcing humanity to adapt in unprecedented ways. The coming decades will determine whether AI remains a tool for prosperity or becomes an uncontrollable force.

Online Publications & Reports

- OpenAI Research Papers – https://openai.com/research
- MIT Technology Review – AI Section – https://www.technologyreview.com/
- Stanford AI Index Report – https://aiindex.stanford.edu/ AI is not just a technological advancement—it is a revolution redefining humanity's place in the digital age. Its presence is felt in every aspect of life, from the way we work to the way we interact, reshaping the very fabric of society. Understanding AI means understanding the future, and those who harness its potential will shape the course of history. The evolution of AI is not just a technical shift; it is a societal transformation. Throughout history, we have witnessed how revolutions in technology reshape civilization—from the steam engine to the internet. AI follows this trajectory, with the potential to redefine what it means to be human. Every industry, from healthcare to finance, is being disrupted, forcing humanity to adapt in unprecedented ways. The coming decades will determine whether AI remains a tool for prosperity or becomes an uncontrollable force.

Influential AI Thinkers & Contributors

- **Geoffrey Hinton, Yoshua Bengio, Yann LeCun** – Pioneers of Deep Learning
- **Elon Musk, Sam Altman, Demis Hassabis** – AI Innovators and Thought Leaders
- **Timnit Gebru, Joy Buolamwini** – AI Ethics and Bias Researchers AI is not just a technological advancement—it is a revolution redefining humanity's place in the digital age. Its presence is felt in every aspect of life, from the way we work to the way we interact, reshaping the very fabric of society. Understanding AI means understanding the

future, and those who harness its potential will shape the course of history. The evolution of AI is not just a technical shift; it is a societal transformation. Throughout history, we have witnessed how revolutions in technology reshape civilization—from the steam engine to the internet. AI follows this trajectory, with the potential to redefine what it means to be human. Every industry, from healthcare to finance, is being disrupted, forcing humanity to adapt in unprecedented ways. The coming decades will determine whether AI remains a tool for prosperity or becomes an uncontrollable force.

For further reading and updates on AI, explore these sources and stay engaged with ongoing research in the field. AI is not just a technological advancement—it is a revolution redefining humanity's place in the digital age. Its presence is felt in every aspect of life, from the way we work to the way we interact, reshaping the very fabric of society. Understanding AI means understanding the future, and those who harness its potential will shape the course of history. The evolution of AI is not just a technical shift; it is a societal transformation. Throughout history, we have witnessed how revolutions in technology reshape civilization—from the steam engine to the internet. AI follows this trajectory, with the potential to redefine what it means to be human. Every industry, from healthcare to finance, is being disrupted, forcing humanity to adapt in unprecedented ways. The coming decades will determine whether AI remains a tool for prosperity or becomes an uncontrollable force.

--- AI is not just a technological advancement—it is a revolution redefining humanity's place in the digital age. Its presence is felt in every aspect of life, from the way we work to the way we interact, reshaping the very fabric of society. Understanding AI means understanding the future, and those who harness its potential will shape the course of history. The evolution of AI is not just a technical shift; it is a societal transformation. Throughout history, we have witnessed how revolutions in technology reshape civilization—from the steam engine to the internet. AI follows this trajectory, with the potential to redefine what it means to be human. Every industry, from healthcare to finance, is being disrupted, forcing humanity to adapt in unprecedented ways. The coming decades will determine whether AI remains a tool for prosperity or becomes an uncontrollable force.